HAPPINESS DEMYSTIFIED

or, if you prefer:

HOW TO LIVE A HAPPIER LIFE
(It's Not Nearly As Difficult As You May Think)

~ Kevin Unruh ~

BookLocker
Trenton, Georgia

Published by BookLocker.com, Inc., Trenton, Georgia.

Printed on acid-free paper.

BookLocker.com, Inc.
2022

First Edition

Library of Congress Cataloguing in Publication Data
Unruh, Kevin
Happiness Demystified by Kevin Unruh
Library of Congress Control Number: 2022916184

Disclaimer

This book details the author's personal experiences with and opinions about the concept of happiness. The author is not a licensed psychiatrist or psychologist.

The author and publisher are providing this book and its contents on an "as is" basis and make no representations or warranties of any kind with respect to this book or its contents. The author and publisher disclaim all such representations and warranties, including, for example, warranties of merchantability and general recommendations for a particular purpose. In addition, the author and publisher do not represent or warrant that the information accessible via this book is accurate, complete, or current.

The statements made about products and services have not been evaluated by the U.S. government. Please consult with your own licensed professional regarding the suggestions and recommendations made in this book.

Except as specifically stated in this book, neither the author or publisher, nor any authors, contributors, or other representatives will be liable for damages arising out of or in connection with the use of this book. This is a comprehensive limitation of liability that applies to all damages of any kind, including (without limitation) compensatory; direct, indirect, or consequential damages; loss of data, income or profit; loss of or damage to property, and claims of third parties.

You understand that this book is not intended as a substitute for consultation with a licensed professional. Before you begin any change in your lifestyle in any way, you should consider consulting a licensed professional to ensure that you are doing what is best for your situation.

This book provides content related to suggestions regarding how to improve one's level of happiness. As such, use of this book implies your acceptance of this disclaimer.

Other Books by the Author

Ethics, Reason, and Excellence:
A Simple Formula for Leadership

To my brother and sister

Contents

Foreword... xiii

Introduction.. 1

Chapter 1: *Change and The Formula* 7

Chapter 2: *Purpose* 13

Chapter 3: *Courage*.. 17

Chapter 4: *Emotional Balance*... 21

Chapter 5: *Kindness and Related Ethics*................................ 25

Chapter 6: *Self-Acceptance*.. 29

Chapter 7: *Self-Awareness* 39

Chapter 8: *Objectivity*.. 43

Chapter 9: *Communication* 47

Chapter 10: *Romantic Relationships* 55

Chapter 11: *Passive-Aggressive Behavior*.............................. 63

Chapter 12: *Procrastination* 67

Chapter 13: *Anger*.. 71

Chapter 14: *Decision-Making Made Easy*.............................. 75

Chapter 15: *Regret* 81

Chapter 16: *Apologies*.. 85

Chapter 17: *Stagnation and Burn-Out*................................... 87

Chapter 18: *Less Philosophy, More...Something* 95

Chapter 19: *Loneliness* 99

Chapter 20: *Forgiveness* 103

Chapter 21: *Boundaries* 109

Chapter 22: *Counseling: Client Psychology* 117

Chapter 23: *A Personal Chapter* 121

Chapter 24: *Self-Help* 127

Chapter 25: *Character and Kids* 131

Chapter 26: *Leaders and Guilt* 137

Chapter 27: *The Only Thing You Can Be* 141

Chapter 28: *Grief and Healing* 145

Chapter 29: *Depression, Suicide, and Suicide Prevention* 151

Chapter 30: *Hard Times* 157

Chapter 31: *The Benefits of Adversity* 159

Chapter 32: *Perseverance* 163

Chapter 33: *Pride, Honesty, and Peace of Mind* 165

Chapter 34: *Gratitude* 169

Chapter 35: *Holes in The Formula* 173

Chapter 36: *A Salve for Emotional Pain* 175

Chapter 37: *Free Bonus Chapter!* 179

Conclusion 185

Acknowledgements 187

Notes 189

Written Guarantee: Assertiveness 193

Written Guarantee: Procrastination 195

If you want to change the world, pick up your pen and write.[1]
– Martin Luther

Foreword

I was very flattered and pleased that Kevin asked me to review his writings, provide feedback, and write the foreword for his latest book. There aren't too many people with the knowledge, wisdom, and insight he has, so when someone like him asks for your assistance, you get very focused, you activate the most philosophical depths of your brain, and you get ready to do some deep-diving into the workings of the mind and human nature.

Discussions with Kevin Unruh are *always* stimulating, amusing, and insightful. He mostly likes to talk about important philosophical concepts and always wants to know what *you* think, welcoming the analysis of others for greater philosophical understanding. To help you get to know the author a little better, I would like to provide the following paragraphs as my official *Foreword* to his book.

Kevin Unruh has been a wise man since I first met him 30 years ago when we both began working on our Master's degrees in counseling. Kevin was a guy who was not afraid to ask the hard questions in class or to offer a perspective that most of the rest of the class hadn't even considered. His level of understanding of the human psyche always struck me as unusual even among the crowd we were in.

It didn't take long for he and I to start talking after class about life, philosophy, psychology, the future, and the nature of human beings in general. He shared insights in some of these discussions, many of which still ring true today and that have returned to my mind many times over the years. He definitely wasn't your typical Master's-level student, but then, I am not sure I was either, which is probably why we enjoyed talking to each other as much as we did and paired up together on numerous class projects. This guy was clearly focused, dedicated, and had the ability to make things happen both in graduate school and otherwise. I always knew he would be successful in many ways as he moved forward.

As the years went by, we went down different-yet-similar career paths and kept in touch, both finding ourselves working with people in diverse and challenging situations with the opportunity to learn from each of those interactions over many years. It's a funny thing. When you are friends with someone you genuinely like and respect, it doesn't really matter when the last time was you saw them or sat down face-to-face. You just pick up where you left off and engage like you always have with ease. That is how it has always been with Kevin.

A few years ago, when Kevin sent me a copy of his previous book, Ethics, Reason, and Excellence: *A Simple Formula for Leadership*, I was excited to read it, especially as a manager of counselors, as I thought it might give me even greater access, in book form, to his leadership experiences and insights. It did that very thing. I read it through in one sitting and made notes as I went. It was excellent material – concepts I use today and have many times since the initial reading. Kevin does not say things casually, so his words are never just a collection of random thoughts or content meant to take up a page or to support an ego. The person I know in Kevin Unruh is humble but adamant and simply wants to share what he knows in order to help others.

I am, by nature, very skeptical about things written or spoken and a very "hard sell" on many things, if not most. This skeptical nature and many years of working in various challenging mental health settings will do that to a person. The material Kevin offers in the present book, however, was very easy for me to "buy," and I am all in. He has put great thought and contemplation into each chapter because he is the kind of person who weighs and measures *everything* before putting pen to paper. This is exceptionally good information that he is sharing in this book, and based on my many years of experience in counseling and mental health care, I am happy to say that I am in complete agreement with what you are about to read.

This book is a superb read with material that will undoubtedly guide you in your quest for happiness. Each premise covered in this book is very important. Each chapter discusses an area of life that is key to your happiness. All the chapters are interrelated and build upon each other. I encourage you to read each chapter and to then give the words some additional thought beyond your initial reading. You *can* be happy, and this book provides practical guidance, direction, and a formula for achieving it. Happiness is rarely achieved if you are nothing more than driftwood being washed down the stream without direction, waiting on happenstance to determine your course, and the philosophies in this book – if you will use them – can act as rudder to help you steer and move toward the destination we all want to reach: *Happiness*.

I challenge you to start the book and give it a thorough read. You will be hard-pressed not to get value from what has been written here. In these pages is an assemblage of gifted insight and many years of wisdom, experience, and learning. I am confident you will not be disappointed and will find yourself thinking back to passages and chapters as reference points as you move forward in the days ahead on your journey to finding your own happiness.

Shaun Manning LPC, NCC
Licensed Professional Counselor
National Certified Counselor

Introduction

Since my teens, I have been searching for *anchors* in life – answers and truths that are universal, immutable, and trustworthy – for the most elemental aspects of why things work out well in this life and for philosophies that both explain successful living and which provide wise and logical principles by which to navigate it. And because of this decades-long search and what I have learned from it, I have come to view the experience of living life – living it *well* – in terms of simple *formulas,* representative of these anchors and truths, that now serve as the faithful guidance that makes my life (and others) easier, happier, and better.

I did not set out to write a book on happiness. All I *set out* to do about two years ago was write a few short essays, in my role as an employee assistance program manager where I work, that I thought might help a few people here and there. After I had written five to seven of these essays, posted them on our internal webpage, and received some positive comments, I wrote a few more and felt badly that I had not written any before this, in that I was quickly made aware from numerous comments by those that had read these essays that they were of genuine value to them. After I had written 15 or so, and co-workers informed me that they had passed them on to others where they work as well as to family members and that these essays had impacted them in compelling and meaningful ways, I realized that this was something I really should be doing on a regular basis. After I had written about *25* essays, I decided that it was probably worthwhile to expound on many of them and to put them all into a book, so that there would be a one-stop shop for anyone trying to improve themselves and the quality of their lives. My initial objective in writing the first few essays was simply to try to be helpful by offering up some perspectives on various psychological and philosophical aspects of life and work; my objective in writing this book, however, was to create an inclusive and practical guide for people to use in endeavoring to determine their own peace and happiness.

1

As an aside, I should tell you that the above paragraph has been re-worked many times, and all because of my good friend Joe. I had asked Joe to read an early draft of the book, and although he made several valuable recommendations, his most adamant contention was that I had severely down-played the impact of my essays in saying, as I wrote above, that I had "received some positive comments." He was annoyed with me for being "too humble," as he ranted kindly but stubbornly about my need to tell the reader, for the purpose of securing more people's interest, that the essays I had written had helped far more people than was implied by the "modest" phrasing in my earlier draft. Later, when I told him that I had revised the draft and had included his *other* recommendations but that I was still uncomfortable with changing the "positive-comments" part and extolling the influence of my own writings, he exasperatingly replied that this "is the most important revision you need to make!" I laughed and told him I just didn't feel comfortable with touting my own work, which provoked the following humorous and frustrated responses: "When are you going to stop being stupid?"; "I think you're just being difficult"; and, "What is wrong with you?" After I stopped laughing, I explained that I was very concerned about being "off-putting" in the opening lines of the book by sounding as though I was bragging on myself. Joe, being a very reasonable man, said that he understand this concern and that my rebuttal was a good one – and then proceeded to fire off this response: "But, you're a writer, so figure it out." This friendly banter continued for a while, and I finally conceded that I would revise that paragraph more to his liking (as it reads now) and then asked him, sarcastically, if he would be satisfied with my stating that my essays had "profoundly changed the lives of at least 10,00 people." His three-word retort was "On the low-side…" So, there you go. Hopefully, my blaming Joe for this absolves me of any culpability in sounding conceited. With that little tale, the pressure is back on both of us – me *and* Joe – so I hope this book delivers.

Living life well – living it successfully, efficiently, productively, and, most importantly, *happily* – is rather simple in my opinion. Life isn't always *easy* – in fact, it *often* isn't – but I believe fervently that if one follows various sound principles for living, it truly can be quite simple. The purpose of this book, therefore, is to discuss these basic principles for living life well, to examine a simple formula that leads to productive and happy living, and to do so in a very straightforward way, in short chapters that are unlikely, I believe, to require much pouring over, in depth study, or re-reading. My goal in this is completely singular: *I just want to help.* I care nothing about being an "author," and I don't care one *whit* about making any money from this. In fact, I can all but guarantee that 98% of the books "sold" will be sold *to me* and then given away for the purpose of getting this message out to anyone willing to read a few pages. I'm sure my publisher loves hearing this…

This was never intended to be an "academic" book. It has some academic aspects to it, naturally, but the following chapters are based solely on my own personal observations and experiences over the last 30 years, give or take – experiences and observations I have made in many different roles as a counselor, advisor, employee assistance program manager, mentor, consultant, educator, friend, co-worker, brother, son, amateur philosopher, and otherwise obsessive/compulsive thinker. I have included no research to validate my beliefs, but I suspect there is likely research out there that supports many, if not most, of them. What I am sharing in this book are philosophies and recommendations that I have seen validated in countless instances in the lives of those whom I have advised, mentored, or counseled, and, of course, that which I have seen validated in my own life, time and again. In short, everything I have written here I sincerely believe to be both inherently and demonstrably true.

In the many years that I have served in the varying roles mentioned above, I have had thousands of meetings with people and have observed, first-hand, that the principles espoused in this book are successful in the lives of just about everyone, whenever they are applied earnestly and consistently. In endeavoring to provide what I believe are real answers to many of life's difficulties, I have written chapters in this book that address many of the most common dilemmas people encounter in life and the mindsets and emotions that go along with them. I have seen these philosophies and life-strategies prove themselves true and successful in literally hundreds of instances – in the lives of those that follow them, and even in those that just try them out on a whim. In fact, there have been many, many people over the years who have told me that the recommendations I have given them, all based on the principles contained herein – despite what was often their initial reluctance, anxiety, and skepticism – "worked just like you said they would..."

I am confident that most of you, like these individuals, will find that the perspectives and principles in these chapters provide practical insights to life's many concerns and that these insights really can bring about genuine resolution, true happiness, and lasting peace of mind for those willing to embrace and apply them. I hope in reading this book you will find, or soon come to believe, that its contents are not only valid but are also easy to incorporate in that all that is required is *will*. But if you are skeptical, if you believe that this is just a collection of biased philosophies from some guy that thinks that successful, peaceful, and happy living can be distilled into one simple formula, I would ask you with nothing but goodwill in my heart to *not* take my word for it. Really, *don't*. After you have read this book, or as you are reading it, mentally examine the lives of others. With a sincere and open mind, look at people with whom you are relatively familiar and see if – regarding those you know who are unhappy in life – see if they apply the principles in this book. I can all but assure you they do not. And, then, try it the other way. Look at those people you know that *are* happy and see if you don't find that most of these people live by these very same principles on a daily basis. I am completely confident that you will not find a single example of contradiction on *either* side of your observations. I have looked, *in earnest,* for such contradictions with an eye for making any necessary revisions to my philosophies, and I have yet to find one. *Not one.*

If *you* are already happy, then *please pass the word* – let people in on *your* system and *your* formula. My bet is that if you are truly happy, your formula is very much the same as mine. But, if you are *unhappy* – regardless of the circumstances – the logical thing to do is to consider making some changes. Sometimes, we need to change our circumstances and, sometimes, we need to change ourselves (i.e., the way we are believing, thinking, reacting, perceiving, interpreting, and so on). Changing our circumstances or ourselves both require mindfulness, humility, discipline, and a *willingness* to change – without them, wise philosophy and sound principles are just ideas… just empty words on a page. If a person is willing to change their current way of thinking, and, in turn, their way of reacting and feeling and navigating life, those experiences in life that were once negative – that were once unsuccessful, unproductive, disillusioning, debilitating, and many other verbs with a connotation of disruption – can become experiences that are positive, fruitful, rewarding, heartening, and peaceful. There are answers in this book, and they are simple. And because they are simple, they are also very easy to understand.

If you are unhappy in even just one area of your life, I believe this book can help you. In fact, I *know* it can. All you need is an open mind and a willingness to give it a try.

Chapter 1

Change and The Formula

"But that's just how I am..." How many times have you heard someone say this? How many times have *you* said it? I suspect most all of us have said this at one time or another, and I can certainly understand why, in that it would be foolish of me to contend that there is not a genetic or biological component to whom we are. *Of course, there is.* In fact, there are *many* ways in which we humans are predisposed to certain feelings and behaviors, and we can all think of examples in ourselves and in others as to how we know this to be true. But, I'm also sure that most of you are also at least *somewhat* familiar with the age-old debate of *nature* vs. *nurture*. That is, *nature* says we are "born with" certain patterns of personality and behavior, and *nurture* says these patterns are influenced by the things that we have *learned* through the process of our upbringing and our external environment. Many, *many* studies have been conducted into this dichotomy, and it is safe to say that when it comes to human behavior, *both* have been found to be influential (the same is also true in animal behavior, incidentally). The point of this is that *how* and *whom* we are is a function of three very distinct things: 1) genetic coding, 2) the way we *learn* to live our lives, and 3) the way we *choose* to live our lives. In this chapter, I want to discuss the sense we have, from time to time, that we are *fated* to think, feel, and behave a certain way due to the notion that our genetics "make" it so. And while I absolutely know that it very often *feels* this way, we are *not* predestined to be one thing or another.

Yes, of course, the traits we inherit from our parents influence our own personality, but they don't set them in stone. If your mother was "the nervous type," for example, there is a fair chance you could be, too. If your father had difficulty focusing on tasks, it is very possible you will also exhibit the same tendencies. Heredity is *often* going to be at play, but anxiety and lack of focus can also be learned traits. In fact, your parents may have learned these from *their* parents. The good thing is that when humans learn something, especially a trait or behavior that is not particularly healthy, it is also possible to *un*-learn it and to rehabituate ourselves to a more positive trait or behavior.

Our reactions to things like guilt, stress, conflict, frustration, fear, loneliness, and other generally negative emotions may very well be a response catalyzed by genetics, but it could just as easily be a reaction to the way we "trained" ourselves to be, or how others inadvertently trained us to react to these things over time. Again, I am quick to admit that heredity plays a powerful part in all the things that make up our personalities, but it *guarantees* nothing, and *nothing* is foisted upon us without our say-so. If we don't want to be a worrier, we don't have to be. If we want to be more focused, we can be. All we have to do is make the decision to change and become that which we would rather be.

"But it's really hard to change…" Yes, it is hard, but you are not a stone or a mineral with a fixed and rigid crystalline structure. You are actually more like a length of wood with a *grain*. And because wood is not stone, elements such as heat, water, and pressure, can all change the grain, bending it 90-degrees – even *180-degrees* – with the right amount of effort. *And we are no different.* We all have a very distinct grain – a pattern and a flow to our personalities – but the grain *can* be turned, and in any direction we choose.

When I was young – 11 or 12, maybe – I perceived myself not to be very mechanically inclined. I saw that other kids knew about building and fixing things, and I thought I just must not have inherited the "mechanical gene," and it bothered me because I thought this seemed like a very useful aptitude to have. Long story short, I *am* relatively mechanically inclined – I just wasn't around too many adults that worked on mechanical things in my earlier years, so I never really learned things like that. So, as an adolescent, I made a concerted effort to learn about mechanical things, and by the time I was in my early-to-mid-20s or so, this aptitude seemed to awaken, and I no longer felt as though I lacked this inclination at all. I'm not saying I could build a suspension bridge without a blueprint or turn a microwave into a cell phone, but I am not as mechanically inept as I feared I was as a kid. All it took was a little effort to rouse the aptitude I already had.

Much more importantly, though, than aptitudes like mechanical ability are the tendencies we have in relation to our *responses to emotions*. Reactions to stress, to anger, to loneliness, to failure, and so on can be learned and inherited just like anything else. But these reactions can be *un-learned,* as well. Now, for those of you that might be complaining to yourself that my example of a mechanical aptitude is not the same as an emotional one, you're right. It's not. So, to make my case a bit more convincing, I should tell you that I did the very same thing with my "predisposition" to worry.

Whether I inherited worry from my mother, who was somewhat prone to worry, or learned it is impossible to say and doesn't really matter, to be frank, because the results are the same. What I *can* say is that I was a worrier in my youth. I disliked that I was a worrier, and I liked it even less when friends would sometimes criticize or tease me for worrying about things. Some of my worry was rooted in general anxiety, but another aspect of my anxiousness was the "borrowing trouble" syndrome that many worriers have – that is, looking for worst-case scenarios that are very unlikely to occur.

As I got older and more introspective and self-aware, I came to dislike this trait/behavior in myself even more so and decided to change it. Instead of conceding to the emotion of anxiety in the form of worry, I nullified it by applying logic. In short, I began to let facts, in conjunction with logical analysis, dictate my thinking so that I could establish a sense of calm and a perspective that removed elements of worry from my perspective. After a few years of trying to create new mental pathways, my tendency to fret went away and has never returned.

Whether you are predisposed to an emotion, you learned it over time from environmental elements, or from a specific individual, your responses to emotions are *not* predestined. You have control over them just as much as you do over which words you choose in a conversation or which color pants you put on before work. Yes, you may be predisposed to choose khaki pants most of the time, but if you want to, you can choose green or blue or brown any day of the week. The majority of the time, we react to *Situation A* exactly like we reacted to *Situation A* in the past. Our emotional reactions in most areas are very much habit-based. But, all we have to do to change our response is to decide how we would *rather* respond and then commit ourselves to rehabituation. Reframing and starting new habits is very simple and it works for anyone of any age. The problem is that adults typically don't have mentors of their own who can guide them in a way similar to the way parents guide and mentor children. Which is one of the reasons counselors were invented. Counselors are not *required*, of course, but they can often help. If you find learning to reframe and rehabituate on your own too difficult, counseling is definitely a good option. But whether it is through self-help or formal counseling, all it takes to trade unhealthy responses and bad habits for healthy ones and better habits is a little focus and commitment.

Life can hand us a lot of difficult stuff, and the fact that we become angry, frustrated, hurt, scared, and so on is often due to the circumstances that we are faced with. But, how we choose to *react* to those circumstances is what dictates how we feel. Obviously, we don't get to choose all of life's circumstances, but far more often than not, how we respond to those circumstances *is* a choice.

You can't get into good physical shape without some exertion. You want to lose weight? You have to put in a little work. You also can't get into good *mental* shape without some exertion. Tired of feeling how you feel? Then choose to feel differently. It's possible – because our emotional responses are *not* pre-coded, and "how you are" is however you *choose* to be. The concept of change is *central* to the concept of my formula for peace and happiness because without a willingness to change, the ability to progress from unhappy to happy is non-existent.

> *Those who cannot change their minds cannot change anything.*[2]
> — George Bernard Shaw

> *If we don't change, we don't grow. If we don't grow,*
> *we aren't really living.*[3]
> — Anatole France

Another very important aspect of change, especially when we are unhappy, is the concept of personal responsibility. *How* we are and *what* we are is defined, more often than not, by choice. We humans *love* to blame various conditions and even other people for our circumstances, which is why counselors, bosses, parents, teachers, and honest friends and family often remind us that *we* need to take responsibility for our own actions. Many times, if not *most* of the time, how we got where we are is not due to bad luck, DNA, or "the world" but is rather due to our own poor decisions, our own imprudent behavior, and our own faulty thought-processes and philosophies. Looking for outside influences to explain our failures is almost always a cop-out and an avoidance of the truth. But we do this because looking inward is unpleasant, and we are afraid that if we really look hard, we might actually *find* the truth – which is that we were at fault all along. But, the good thing about finding the truth – no, the *great* thing – is that *now* we know what we need to change.

So, if one *is* willing to make changes in order to become happier, what next? Well, that's where the formula comes in.

The simple formula that I will use to establish the premise of this book – that emotional peace and happiness can be achieved through application of very specific philosophies and principles – is composed of five interrelated elements: *Purpose, Courage, Emotional Balance, Kindness & Other Ethics, and Self-Acceptance.* That is, to live in peace and harmony with yourself and others, you must 1) have a purpose in life, 2) have courage as you navigate through it, 3) be in command of your own emotions, 4) be kind and ethical, and 5) learn to like yourself as a person. These five elements work. *They do.* If you have these, you will be happy. I am not suggesting that one may not use *other* elements to induce happiness or that happiness can only come through this specific formula. What I am suggesting is that these baseline elements *will* bring about happiness and that those that are happy in this life almost always deliberately embrace this formula, or at least live their lives with this formula running in the background. Though this formula is relatively easy to understand, I would like to give it a bit more perspective. So, let's begin with a discussion of *Purpose*.

Chapter 2

Purpose

If you struggle with maintaining a consistent, long-term state of happiness or contentment, I have a simple question for you that will help in almost all cases. It's deep, but it's very simple. *Ready?*

~~Do you have lots of cash in your pocket or purse?~~
~~Do you have more than 1,000 friends on Facebook?~~
~~Do you have a super-fast red, yellow, green, or orange car?~~
~~Are you taller than the average person, smarter, better looking?~~
~~Do you have a really nice coin collection?~~
~~Do you wear new clothes every season?~~
~~Do you have an underground bunker with lots of doomsday supplies?~~
~~Is your stereo system louder than the teenager's next door?~~
~~Is your 4WD vehicle jacked up higher than everyone else's?~~
~~Did you finally find the perfect shampoo?~~
~~Do your jeans cost more than $150.00?~~
~~Can your dog do more tricks than your mother-in-law's?~~
Do you have a dedicated purpose in life and are you fulfilling it?

The French expression *raison d'être* says it nicely… one's *reason to be* (the Japanese call it *ikigai,* incidentally*).*

Have you decided what you are all about? Have you committed yourself to a primary purpose? Have you decided where you are going in life and why? If you have not found your reason for being, your purpose, *the thing* that best defines your value to those around you, it's important that you eventually work this out if you want to live a life of sustained happiness.

One's purpose in life is obviously very personal. That is, one's purpose should not be influenced by what others may want of you or for you. It also need not be *grand* to be valid, effective, or worthwhile. All it *needs* to be is sincere and you will be happy. And why is this so important? Because every day when you wake up, you will be doing

13

what you care most about and you will know what direction in life you are going. In short, you will know your daily mission.

And just so there is no misunderstanding, I am not talking about the purpose or the meaning *of life* – that is an entirely different discussion, an entirely different book, even – I am only talking here about the purpose of *your* life.

Knowing your life's purpose gives you an identity, but it also attaches you to the world around you and keeps you connected. Whether your purpose is to be the best Mom or Dad, the best coach, the best tailor, or the world's fastest posthole digger doesn't really matter. Generally speaking, if your purpose has value to whatever group of people you care about most *and* you are passionate about doing it, it is a worthy purpose. A good Mom or Dad has just as much value as a good physician, a good farmer, or a good beekeeper. One's life purpose should not, cannot *rightfully* be judged by the world's standard of what is often considered important. It need not have marquee-level prominence to be a truly great purpose, and this isn't a numbers game either (who helps the most people). It's about making a sincere contribution in the field, culture, group, place, or endeavor in which you feel you are best able to add value. And if that means dedicating yourself to being a good parent and raising a good human being – as opposed to being the CEO of a big company, for example – please don't ever think your contribution is any less important. *It isn't.* There is no question in my mind that the world needs far more good parents than it needs CEOs (nothing personal against CEOs, of course).

Regardless of your age – 21 to 101 – if you haven't identified, claimed, and dedicated yourself to the purpose of your life, if you haven't found your *raison d'être*, it is never too late to start looking. And the faster you find it, the happier you will be.

Someone I was talking to not long ago about this asked: "How does one go about figuring out their purpose?" and, "Can a person's purpose change over time?" Well, the answer to the first question is easy: Any true purpose starts with a genuine passion. If you haven't found your purpose yet, start the search with what you are truly passionate about. Then, determine which passion it is (if there is more than one) that brings the most value to those around you. As for your purpose changing, yes, it can change with age or circumstance or epiphany. With aging often comes evolution. As our experiences grow and develop, so, typically, do our philosophies and perspectives and often our priorities. A purpose we thought was our calling at age 25 might not be the same at age 45. It doesn't mean we were wrong at 25. It usually just means we know the world a little better now and, more importantly, a little more about ourselves. The key to knowing when you have it right is the same as when you know you have found the perfect pair of shoes, dress, word, spice, song, mate, etc.: You feel it in your bones. *In your atoms*. The chemistry of *you* coalesces with the chemistry of the *purpose*. You will know when it's right and you will know when it is *no longer* right. And if you have any doubt, then it most likely isn't.

> *You were put on this earth to achieve your greatest self,*
> *to live out your purpose, and to do it courageously.*[4]
> – Steve Maraboli

Of the five elements in the formula for happiness, this is the simplest to understand, in my opinion, so I won't devote any more space to it, but you must have a purpose in life in order to be truly happy, and only *you* can decide what that is.

Now let's discuss the role of *Courage* in happiness.

Chapter 3

Courage

Mohandas Gandhi said, "*Happiness is when what you think, what you say, and what you do are in harmony.*"[5] And Thucydides said, "*The secret of happiness is freedom. The secret of freedom is courage.*"[6] The reason I love these two together is that the latter empowers the former. Courage, therefore, is the linchpin. Courage is *everything*. If you are not happy, it is almost assuredly, at least in part, a function of courage. I will illustrate this with a list of some of the more common reasons that people are unhappy:

- Poor relationships
- Poor work situation
- Poor self-image
- Financial problems
- Lack of friends/companions
- Poor health
- Afraid of telling people how you feel
- Lack of choices

Now let's analyze each of these through the filter of courage:

- Is the bad relationship due to a lack of courage to make changes in yourself that might improve the relationship, or is it because you lack the courage to get *out* of the relationship?
- Same for work: Are you unhappy at work because you aren't the best employee you could be or because you lack the courage to demand a change *or* the courage to leave?
- Do you dislike yourself because you believe yourself to be unsalvageable, or do you simply lack the courage to start making changes to improve whom you are?

- Are your financial problems truly irreversible, or do you lack the courage to make a concerted effort toward repairing things?
- Do you lack friends because there are truly no good people left in the world, or could it be because you lack the courage to make the first move?
- Is your poor health a foregone conclusion, or could it be improved with courage and action?
- Do you *really* have nothing to say, or do you just tell yourself that because you lack the courage to speak your mind?
- Are your choices limited because there are limited choices, or are they limited because you lack the courage to expand the number of choices actually available? Put another way – in the case of a man looking for a mate, for instance – are there so few women available in the world, or are his options merely limited by the number of women he has the courage to speak to? As the saying goes, *"fortune favors the bold..."*[7] (The Aeneid, Virgil).

What allows those few audacious people we all know to speak their mind without hesitation or fear? What allows those quirky friends of ours to "step to the beat of a different drummer"? What allows some people to be the sole minority opinion in the midst of peers who are in the 99.9% majority? The answer to all of these, of course, is *courage*.

All of us have someone in our social group that will have the "hard talk" with a friend. All of us know that one man or woman that we point to when we're in a group and something comes up that requires some level of confrontation. We hear about someone doing something wrong or ill-advised, and we look at each other, and everyone says, "Go get Catherine – she'll talk to him." The Catherines of the world have courage. Those that do not want to talk to the person in question (let's call him "Bill") often do *not* have courage. Often, in fact, the Bills of the world will tell a Catherine that they "talked to everyone and everyone said what I was doing was fine." So why does Catherine say something and the others don't? Because Catherine believes that saying something is more important than letting it go. She believes that confronting Bill is worth the uncomfortableness that comes with the confrontation. Courage gives Catherine the ability to put the situation higher than her own feelings of reluctance. She is able to put responsibility over fear, ethics over *Self*; whereas, the group chose to "agree" with Bill simply because they chose the easier path of non-confrontation.

In situations in which confrontation arises, there is almost always tension. People generally do not like confrontation, and it makes most people very uncomfortable, so to cope with it, most people choose non-confrontation in the form of either agreement ("Yeah, Bill, uh, sure… I see no problem with it…") or avoidance ("Bill, that's up to you. I don't really have an opinion either way…"). Both release the tension posed by the conflict, but both leave us conflicted. In cases where nothing really comes of Bill's bad behavior, the conflict you felt initially evaporates naturally, because the event made no real mark on history. But what about those times when Bill's behavior causes a serious problem? What about the times when someone gets hurt? What happens to the tension and conflict then? Usually, it turns into guilt, and if the event is dire enough, the guilt can easily turn into chronic anxiety and depression. Fear and lack of courage often cause us to do things we regret. *Often.* Sometimes fear and lack of courage become a way of life, a life of coping with tension, dread, and fear over long periods of time by allowing it to beat us into submission – or just looking away so as not to make eye contact…*with ourselves.* Another very insidious and harmful aspect of fear is that it causes us to be lesser than we would otherwise be.

I was talking with someone recently who had developed a reputation for poor responsiveness and they asked me for help. After a very brief discussion, the person told me that they often did not respond immediately to co-workers because they were afraid of providing an answer and receiving a negative reply. Fear, in this instance, gave her the reputation not of being intimidated so much as it did of being discourteous and lazy. This was not accurate or true, but regardless of her intent, the end result was the same: She did not respond to things in a timely way. Lack of courage (fear) is harmful in so many ways. Once fear becomes a habit, it influences almost everything that we do, stealing from us our ethics, our freedom, and what it means to be our truest *Self.*

> *Courage is the most important of all the virtues,*
> *because without courage you can't practice any other virtue*
> *consistently.*[8]
>
> – Maya Angelou

Courage is an immensely powerful thing, and even though you may not have been "born" with a large quotient of it, courage is something you can increase, and it can be increased by simply *having* it. Just like many other things in life, having courage is a choice. You can be fearful one day and courageous the next. All you have to have is the conviction to make the choice.

> *Courage is not the absence of fear; it is acting in spite of it.*[9]
> – Mark Twain

No matter your background, your life experiences, or your personality, courage will come to anyone who has the resolve to invite it in (and the really neat thing about it is that the more you have it, the more you get because *courage begets more courage*). I am not suggesting that it doesn't come easier to some than to others. *Of course, it does.* What I am suggesting is that every individual has the ability to exhibit courage anytime they choose. And once you have courage, you can control your destiny, which naturally leads to the freedom to be whom you want to be. *Which leads to happiness.* To my mind – more than any other attribute we have – *courage* leads us to happiness because it gives us choices, control, and excellence, and all because it gives us freedom. Thucydides could not have been more right. Nor could have Plato...

> *Courage is a kind of salvation.*[10]
> – Plato

And now let's talk about the third element in the formula: *Emotional Balance.*

Chapter 4

Emotional Balance

The first "working title" (for those of you not "in the business," that's super fancy writer speak for "draft") I was going to use for this chapter was "Emotion Management." And even though that *is* what I want to discuss here – the management of one's emotions – I just didn't like the *feel* of "emotion management" as a title, so I changed it to the present one. Both of these titles say what I want to say, but *emotional balance* feels a little cleaner in a sense. But just to make sure the concept is clear, let me take a moment to define "emotional balance" in some detail.

In using the term here, I intend it to depict a sense of balance within the heights and depths that a given emotion *could* take on versus the emotional reactions that would arguably be the most healthy or productive in a given circumstance. For example, on a spectrum, *frustration* could be expressed as very high or very low in a particular context, but *emotional balance,* by my description, represents a *poised* amplitude of frustration which produces, for example, the greatest amount of restraint without being repressive and is the most expressive and cathartic without being self-indulgent or escalating. *Emotional balance* acknowledges and respects emotion but doesn't let it take control. Emotional balance is giving the appropriate amount of energy to an emotion without losing any of its benefits and without getting drawn into any of its negativities.

I suspect it will not be surprising to you to know that, as with many other principles I believe in, the process of managing one's emotions and maintaining emotional balance can be expressed in yet another simple formula, such as the one I have for *achieving* emotional balance:

1. Feel
2. Analyze/Assess (the "data")
3. Feel again (in light of the data)
4. Repeat

I will expound on this sub-formula shortly.

Emotions are very mysterious things. They fascinate me, so I have spent most of my life thinking about them, analyzing them, and trying to devise ways to address them in the most productive ways possible. Here are a few things that I know/believe about them:

Emotions can creep up on us slowly, but they can also hit us hard and fast. There is an aspect of our individual emotional schematic that is hard-wired (we are predisposed to various tendencies with regard to specific emotions), but we also very much *learn* various emotional behaviors and our reactions to those emotions, as we discussed in Chapter 1. Yes, there is a certain innocence and "honesty" that comes with the emotions that a person tends toward (i.e., predisposition), but, emotions – especially how we choose to *react* to and *manage* them – is very much something that is *learned*, which means our reactions to and management of them can also be *un*-learned, altered, and improved, if we have the desire and the will to do so.

At whatever the velocity emotions may manifest in us, they more often than not *seem* to have a will of their own, as if we have no choice in the matter. True, we are the source of our own emotions, but our minds do not always have total control of how, when, or why these emotions *first* appear. Which brings us back to the sub-formula above. The most important part of our emotional life should not be focused or blamed or even *analyzed* so much on the *phase* of an emotion's presence; rather, our focus should be on how we choose to manage it once it appears.

Many people – perhaps *most* even – have a tendency of allowing their emotions to dictate to them how they feel. They tend to say to themselves, consciously or otherwise, *"I feel it; therefore, it is valid."* And, I will be the first to tell you that this perception, this assessment, is reasonable and understandable *in the moment(s) that the emotion first appears*. But the sub-formula I am promoting includes an *immediate* second step, which is to analyze the basis for *why* we feel the way we do, then to assess whether or not how we feel and why is reasonable, healthy, fair, etc. This step is little more than the application of objectivity, which is crucial to determining whether or not what we are feeling is, in fact *reasonable*. The following is a very simplistic example, but hopefully it makes the point.

It is common to experience hurt feelings if you ask someone to look at a painting of yours, for example, and though they tell you they like it very much, they also tell you that there are aspects of it they think could be improved. And even though you asked them to be "brutally honest" with you, for several different reasons, this lack of *perfect* approval can hurt the feelings of the average person. In these situations, what many, if not most, people do is *concede* to these emotions, to indulge the hurt feelings and to give them weight simply because they *are occurring.* In the moment, this is understandable enough, but a much more healthy, productive, and objective way of handling disappointment and hurt, in this example, is to immediately begin evaluating *why* you feel what you feel in order to determine if it is valid *beyond* its initial manifestation. To do this, the logical thing to do is to transition from merely feeling to *thinking* in a very analytical way (Step 2). A quick analysis of the situation could very easily reveal that there are many reasons that a person may not love *every* aspect of your creation, which reasons should be applied to the hurt and disappointment so that these emotions can be viewed in a more reasonable and objective light (Step 3).

First of all, in this example, it is important to remember that you asked for *their* opinion and their opinion is unlikely to perfectly mirror your own (and, of course, as we all know, *"there is no accounting for taste..."*). Further, not loving one aspect of your creation is *not* a rejection of the whole creation – it is merely commentary on *one* aspect. It is also not a rejection of you, the creator. Your critic's lack of complete agreement is also not the same as saying it is not good. Again, it is merely an expression of preference, *not* a condemnation of the quality of your work or of your level of skill. I could go on, but the point is that when we examine *why* we might feel hurt in this situation, it should become clear that the only reason we have become hurt is because we have *chosen* that emotion and not because that emotion has been *assigned* to us by our critic's opinion. Feeling hurt and disheartened are simply not appropriate reactions under these circumstances. They are *real* enough, in that they are happening, but just because they are happening does not necessarily make them rational or true. Objectivity is imperative, here, but, unfortunately, is very difficult to apprehend, especially in the midst of an emotional situation. Which is why asking someone else to *assist* you in the assessment of your feelings is often very helpful. [I discuss more on the topic of objectivity in Chapter 8.]

Emotions should not commandeer us. They may come on with little, if any, conscious invitation, but we are certainly not subject to any prolonged "will" we may tend to attribute to them. *We* control our emotions. *We* decide what to do with them after they show up. *We* choose how long they last and whether they are compelling beyond their first appearance. We are *not* bound by our emotions over time. 1) *Feel; 2) Analyze/Assess; 3) Feel Again; 4) Repeat*: This is a sound formula for putting our emotions in the most logical, healthy, and credible context possible. I am *not* saying the emotion you feel in *Moment 1* is not valid. What I am saying is that this sub-formula allows you to take *Moments 2, 3,* and *4* and sublimate them (your emotions) with greater context and a broader, more enlightened perspective so that your emotions may become more realistic, more manageable, less stressful, and less disruptive. I am *not* anti-emotion; I simply believe in bringing our emotions to a presence in which they are experienced in the most unbiased and well-reasoned state possible. *This* is emotional balance.

The sign of an intelligent people is their ability to control emotions by the application of reason.[11]

– Marya Mannes

Now, I would like to discuss one of my very favorite topics and the fourth element of the happiness formula: *Kindness and Related Ethics.*

Chapter 5

Kindness and Related Ethics

There are great powers in this world of ours. But many times, the greatest power comes not from those things that we humans have *contrived* to be powerful but rather from those things that are natural: the wind, the ocean, fire, the earth, weather, human ingenuity, the human spirit, beauty, and many others, of course. And though not spoken of in the same class typically, *kindness* is another of these immensely powerful things – as powerful as just about anything on this planet. This commentary is *not* about morality, for those that may be anticipating my taking this chapter in that direction. It is simply a reminder of the tremendous power that we have the privilege of being able to wield every day. Power that benefits each of us as much as others – in the form of kindness.

Kind people are *happy* people (it may also be as true that happy people are kind people, but I am not as confident in this assertion – not because I doubt it, per se – but merely because I am just not as certain). What I *am* certain about is that truly kind people are happy. But first, let me tell you what I think makes someone "kind."

Kindness, to me, is many things. It is goodwill towards others, compassion, helpfulness, generosity, courtesy, thoughtfulness, concern, friendliness, and sincerity. But the most important aspect of kindness, as I define it, is that *true* kindness is *a way of life*.

In speaking to many people on this topic, I have found that when someone's kindness is questioned, their defense is often either cosmetic or parsing and selective, for instance, that they "always say please and thank you" or that they "give to charity" or that many of their friends have told them "how nice" they are (but as Steven Sondheim astutely noted, "Nice is different than good"[12]). But these defenses are almost always just patches, compensations or mitigations for behavior that is otherwise *not* so nice. For these people, "nice" and "kindness" are buzz words, or rating levels, as it were, which they believe they can earn by way of individual acts. But true kindness is *not* this way. *True* kindness is a spirit that permeates and guides one's words and deeds throughout the day. It is a *commitment* and not just a series of adjectives or acts. *Truly* kind people wake every morning with the *intention* of being kind, of *living* their kindness. For these people, it is a philosophy, a belief system, and an integral part of their personal culture.

Truly kind people are happy because kindness is good and because it tends to beget more kindness. It gladdens people. It inspires people. It *moves* people within and often incites them to repeat the kindness they were shown. Kindness is an easy and excellent gift to give. It costs nothing, has an immediate impact, is self-propagating, and gives us hope. Kindness causes people to smile, to like us, and to reflect the kindness back, now making the *giver* of kindness the recipient of it. I could give example after example of how kindness does all these things, but the concept is so intuitive, so obvious to all (it *is* obvious, isn't it?), that to presume to illustrate the point further by citing such instances would not likely serve my purpose any better.

An aspect of kindness that perhaps *does* deserve greater emphasis, however, is the kindness done to strangers and to those you may not agree with or who don't agree with you. *All* kindness is good, but kindness to strangers, and to those with whom we may not always be "in sync," perhaps, is the most powerful kind of all.

Kindness to family and friends is a very good thing and it is certainly no less valuable than kindness done to those we do not know. But what makes kindness to strangers particularly powerful is that it is unexpected and, when done in its purest form, is done merely for the sake of doing it. Kindness to those we care about doesn't have an "agenda," per se, but it more often than not has its various promptings. Whether tradition (birthday gifts, for example), or just routine expressions of affection, the familiar recipient in these cases is generally not surprised by our kindness. But with strangers – other than the self-congratulatory, self-impressed "kindnesses" that people sometimes perpetrate (making a minor spectacle of giving up one's seat on a subway or plane, or announcing for all to hear that you are letting someone ahead of you in line at the grocery store, for example) –

spontaneous kindness, kindness with no ulterior motive whatsoever, is the highest form of kindness there is, I think, in that, other than gratitude, there is really no particular benefit to the giver. Without agenda, without motive, without expectation, and with nothing but a selfless heart, *this* gift of kindness conveys the earnest message that this act is completely and absolutely for the other person and nothing more. In a hurried and harried world where self-absorption is often commonplace, acts of kindness to those who can do nothing for us in return is supremely powerful.

> *What wisdom can you find that is greater than kindness?*[13]
> – Jean-Jacques Rousseau

Being kind to others is a wonderful, compassionate thing and is the most inexpensive of our most valuable gifts. Kindness to strangers, merely for the sake of it, is even more wonderful and even more powerful because it tells the person that, even though I don't know you, I care how you *feel*, I care how you *are*, and I care that we inhabit the same space, no matter how large that space may be. Life is sometimes a tough place to live. Kindness to others gladdens the heart, brightens the spirit, engenders hope, and acknowledges to the recipient – whether we know them or not – that we are all in this together and that goodwill is being extended their way.

> *The first step in the evolution of ethics is a sense of solidarity with other human beings.*[14]
> – Albert Schweitzer

Although kindness is not typically included in a traditional discussion of *ethics*, it is no less an "ethic" to my mind than is honesty or fairness, for example. And, while I happen to believe that kindness is one of the most important ethics a person can follow, there are many other important ethical principles, of course, that bring about happiness in people, as well.

As noted, honesty and fairness are two such ethical principles. And even if a person cared nothing about the moral aspects of these, it would be very difficult to argue that being honest and fair do not help one to be happy. Besides the fact that honesty and fairness just *feel* right and are universally considered to *be* right, these two principles also cause people to trust us, to respect us, and to like us – all of which tend to bring us happiness. I think it is safe to say, without enumerating each and every ethic we humans commonly observe, that most all ethical behavior elicits positive reactions in others, and, in turn, positive reactions, and affirming treatment by others tends to produce happiness in us. But before I end the discussion on "related ethics," I want to give another endorsement to the element of *"The Formula"* that is important when it comes to these other ethics, and no one has ever said it better, in my opinion, than Maya Angelou. As you can see, I love this quote so much, I have included it a second time...

Courage is the most important of all the virtues, because without courage you can't practice any other virtue consistently.[8]
– Maya Angelou

Although as we discussed in Chapter 3 that courage is essential to our ability to achieve freedom, it is just as important to our ability to be good and kind. Yes, courage gives us the power to be free of many, many negative things, but it also gives us the power to choose to be exactly what and how we want to be. Without it, we become subject to the external influences of people and the internal influences of insecurity, all influences that we allow to betray whom we really are. There is *so much* power in courage. There is no question in my mind that it is, *in fact*, the most important of all the virtues. It is a philosophy in and of itself, and like kindness – for all its many and great benefits – I believe courage should also be a way of life and not just a word in a list of virtues. Courage is always powerful, but it is even more powerful when it becomes a habit. In fact, I can say this unequivocally about courage: As my courage has increased over the years, so has the quality of my life and the depth and breadth of my happiness.

Let's now finalize the formula with the last of the five elements: *Self-Acceptance.*

Chapter 6

Self-Acceptance

There are many reasons people find themselves unhappy with life: financial problems, relationship problems, existential issues, health concerns, work, anxiety, depression, and loneliness, for example. But all of these problems are bearable, reparable, even *preventable*, in my opinion, if one has a strong foundation in self-acceptance and self-esteem. Although there can be many aspects and avenues for changing our self-image for the better, one of the primary ways that is well within all of our abilities to address is one that comes with a very simple solution: To become more likable, we should *do* things and *be* things that are worthy of likability. If you have poor self-esteem because you don't like yourself very well, and if you don't like yourself very well because you aren't particularly likable in one or more areas, then the obvious remedy is to take action to improve in those areas.

For example, if you're in a bad mood much of the time, it would be wise to make a sincere effort to determine why and work to resolve the issue. Have a history of difficulty in getting along with people? Seems like it would be a good idea to evaluate why that is and do what it takes to mend the problem. Having trouble with your boss? Let's first ask if you are an excellent employee. If not, *become* excellent, and let's see if the trouble you have had with your boss doesn't dissipate on its own. Poor body image? If you can change what you don't like about your body, then why not *change what you don't like about your body*. And if you cannot change it due to the nature of what you do not like (height, shoe size, or anything else that is, for the most part, impossible or very difficult to change), *acceptance* of these aspects is absolutely critical.

If you are having problems in these areas or in any others, it is always wise to look inwardly, first. Self-acceptance – having a good self-image and good self-esteem – is often proportional to how much we like ourselves and how much we like ourselves is very often proportional to how much we are liked by others. Sometimes, the simple act of trying to improve ourselves – specifically our *conduct* as a member of the human race – can improve our level of self-acceptance and self-satisfaction. I always start there, and I recommend the same to others. Of course, when the physical self is involved – you don't like your size 14 foot, for example – there is no "improvement" to be made, so all you can do is learn to accept what you cannot change. *"That's easy for you to say,"* someone might be thinking. Well, yes it is, actually, because the only other option – to lament your unchangeable shoe size – is not an option at all – at least not one with any foreseeable resolution.

Because true belonging only happens when we present our authentic, imperfect selves to the world, our sense of belonging can never be greater than our level of self-acceptance...[15]

– Brené Brown

Sometimes, however, a lack of self-acceptance is baffling. Sometimes, people that *are* quite likeable do not like themselves very much, and it is difficult for others to understand why. While the origins of this mysterious kind of self-esteem problem are different from those *un*-mysterious kinds discussed above, *this* kind needs resolving just as much as the other, because no matter how you slice it, *something* is causing you not to like yourself (a discussion of possible origins of self-esteem and insecurity issues will be discussed shortly). And no matter what the reason or origin, if you do not like yourself, you will not have good self-esteem and you will, therefore, never be truly happy. The formula for happiness has five parts, five important foundational elements, but without this one – *self acceptance* – the other four are very unlikely to matter. That's right. If you were to press me on which of the five is the most crucial, I would have to say self-acceptance (self-esteem, self-regard, self-respect).

Over many years of observation, I have come to believe that people with 1) a defined life purpose, 2) inner courage, 3) the ability to manage one's emotions, 4) a strong sense of kindness and related ethics, and 5) genuine self-acceptance are rarely unhappy. If you don't want to take my word for it, that is perfectly OK – skepticism is often healthy – but, please put these assertions to the test before you dismiss them as the adamant declarations of a slightly eccentric, bearded guy in a plaid shirt with a weird last name (no, not the dude you saw last night in the parking lot – *me*).

If you can give me an example of an unhappy person that has all five of these *and* is free from an unfortunate chemical imbalance (e.g., depression, bipolarism, etc.) or a major physical health concern, I would be very interested in hearing the details. Otherwise, I am confident you will find that people *with* all the elements of the formula are, in fact, content and happy. And, even when things *don't* go their way, even if they *do* happen to have an unfortunate biochemical problem or a significant health concern, they *still* remain generally satisfied and at peace with their circumstances, overall. Yes, life can and often does deal us bad cards – there is no question about that – but, true happiness is not typically affected in the long-term by negative life conditions, unless we allow it to be. And, on the chance that the logic of this claim is not as readily apparent as I think it is, I will expound a bit more.

Self-esteem is one of the most important components of mental health there is, perhaps the very *most* important. And one might say that "mental health" is just another word for "happiness." So, it is not too difficult to see that self-esteem plays a large part in our individual happiness.

Self-esteem is an interesting and often confounding psychological construct. Some people are just *born* with naturally good self-esteem (we've all seen the little boy or girl who seems to jump out of the womb with a "Look-at-me-world – *watch-me-work*" attitude). But, self-esteem is also something that tends to be nurtured by our parents and other loved ones. It can also be *damaged* by these same people, as many of you unfortunately know, putting us on a shaky foundation from the outset, a foundation that is often difficult to "outgrow." But, however we may come by our quotient of high, low, or medium self-esteem, I think most of us can agree that it is directly proportional to our level of happiness.

Based on personal experience and first-hand observations, I have found that low self-esteem generally falls into four categories of origination:1) genetic predisposition; 2) unhealthy relationships; 3) incongruity between how you perceive yourself and how you really are (e.g., perceiving yourself as unsuccessful in life, when your "life résumé" clearly demonstrates the opposite), and 4) guilt (disappointment, shame, embarrassment) from conducting one's self in a manner indicative of something less than one's potential. All of these are tied to our self-image. When we don't like ourselves, we will be insecure and have poor self-esteem. So, the trick, regardless of how we may come to perceive ourselves poorly, is to learn to do the opposite. Luckily, we can learn to overcome all of the four above, but it takes a little work. Predispositions and lifelong habits have formed pathways in our thinking that do not get re-mapped overnight – but it doesn't take forever, either.

Let's discuss insecurity a bit more.

"Have you talked to Richard, lately? It seems like he has been sulking a lot…"
"Oh, he's just insecure…"

"Hey, Kim, have you noticed how snippy Charlotte has been the last few days?"
"Oh, you know Charlotte, she's just insecure…"

"What do you think the deal is with Ed?"
"Look, he's very insecure, so he's sensitive about everything…"

Insecurity is a subject that comes up in many, many conversations about people, regardless of the circles we may be in. It is so common, in fact, it is almost a default "diagnosis" of just about anyone that is discomforted by one emotion or another. And while *insecurity* may be something that appears to be over-diagnosed at times, it is, in my estimation, very often quite accurate. Insecurity *is* very common and is very often the source of negative emotions and poor self-esteem in *a lot* of people.

Because we live among other humans who critique us on our appearance, behaviors, clothing, jobs, children, cars, yards, *etc.*, *etc.*, *etc.*, insecurities are rampant, especially in this age of social media. Humans are tough critics. *Very* tough and often harsh. And all humans know this, so the average human tends to be concerned about being judged harshly, unfairly, or just critically, which causes said humans to be insecure. If we humans lived alone on deserted islands, there would be little to no insecurity, I am almost certain. But, we don't, so insecurity comes, for the most part, from being part of a society. Yes, it is theoretically possible, I suppose, to be insecure *independent* of our concerns about societal judgments, but it is not common enough, in my opinion, to be worthy of discussion in this particular chapter. The point is, we have insecurities because we are part of a group, usually *many* groups, in one form or another, and feeling scrutinized by these groups can cause anxiety and insecurity in just about anyone who does not possess a strong sense of self-acceptance and self-esteem. So, what is the key to ridding ourselves of insecurities, increasing our self-esteem, and achieving self-acceptance? Remember the mantra: *Do* and *be* things that will cause you to be likable.

I have said this to many a parent over the years as it relates to children and self-esteem, and I said it for the first time to my sister about 25 years ago as she was beginning to raise her first child: *"One of the most important jobs of a parent is to raise your child in a way that causes the world to like her."* Because when the world (your co-workers, your friends, your family, your bosses, etc.) likes you, you will, far more often than not, have good self-esteem, and good self-esteem tends to make one happy. Yes, I understand that circumstances outside our control can cause us to be unhappy, but how we react to those circumstances is how we are judged, and those with unfortunate circumstances are not necessarily given over to poor self-esteem. Poor self-esteem tends to arise when we *react* poorly to negative circumstances, as if those circumstances are an *excuse* for negative behavior. And, yes, if you are curious, my sister (and brother-in-law) *did* raise their first child in a way that caused the world to like her. As they did their second and third child [insert proud uncle emoji here].

I knew a young woman some years ago who was chronically insecure, and for all the years I knew her in our younger days, she walked around with what appeared to be bitterness or some form of a grudge. She was smart, attractive, had a good sense of humor (when one could cajole it from her), a good childhood (I knew the family), and from all appearances, was a person anyone would have assumed would be as happy as or happier than anyone else. After years of odd and very avoidant and negative behavior, I asked her very directly one evening when we were in college why she was so unhappy.

After hours of conversation and many tears later, she was finally able to tell me that she was angry because she was constantly afraid of rejection. She explained that when she was in her early teens, a boy had rejected her and she never really recovered from it. Instead of realizing that it had far less to do with her than it did with him, she internalized it and decided that she must be "ugly" or "dumb" or in some other way unworthy of his affections; otherwise, she would not have been rejected, as she perceived things. Because this was such a traumatizing event for this young woman, she quickly began avoiding contact with boys and other situations in which she might have to deal with rejection. This lasted into her late teens, which is when I spoke to her about it. She told me that although she knew that it was mostly subconscious, she realized that by being in a bad mood and looking disinterested in people, by scowling, and not encouraging relationships with men *or* women, she could keep from feeling rejection because she was rarely approached in a social way by anyone. It was a classic case of rejecting others before they could reject her.

As most of us know, people with body dysmorphic disorder have a distorted and irrational perception of their body. But people can *also* have a distorted perception of whom they are and how they are perceived by others, just like the young woman above did. Her distorted self-perception caused her years of insecurity, sadness, and even self-resentment, and she was unable to enjoy relationships, or even *have* relationships, for being in constant fear of rejection. The very first thing that helped her turn the corner is that she was willing to identify what the problem was. Then, she was willing to work on resolving those feelings and perceptions that were irrational until the fear of rejection was replaced with a willingness to give things another try. I bumped into this woman many years later at a restaurant, where I found her to be happily married, genuinely cheerful, and pleasantly confident.

If you are experiencing insecurities and low self-esteem, first ask yourself if you are doing everything you can in your life to be a likable person. If you are, then perhaps you are *predisposed* to poor self-esteem and might benefit from consultation with a mental health counselor and/or physician. If you *can* make improvements in your daily behaviors, it is worthwhile to try to make those improvements, wherever those might be needed, and to see if making an effort to become a better person (whatever that might mean to you), a better family member, or a better employee, for example, doesn't cause a positive change in the way you are perceived and treated by others. I will be shocked if it doesn't.

Life definitely deals us all different cards, but, long-term happiness and self-esteem, which are very often inextricably linked, are not affected by negative circumstances and life conditions unless we allow them to be. As we have discussed, self-image and self-esteem are often proportional to how much we like ourselves and how much we like ourselves is very often proportional to how much we are liked by others. Sometimes, the simple act of trying to improve ourselves, specifically our conduct as a member of the human race, can improve our self-esteem.

If you have purpose, courage, emotional balance, live an ethical life, have real self-acceptance and you suffer a financial set-back, for example, *courage* and *emotional balance* usually prop you up and give you the confidence to know that you will find a way to work things out (*self-esteem* does the very same thing here, but comes at it from a different angle). If you lose your job, no fault of your own, *purpose, emotional balance,* and *self-acceptance* work together to assure you that you know where you belong in this life and have the talent and skills to get there. When a relationship ends (again, no fault of your own), *self-acceptance* and *emotional balance* reaffirm that sometimes things just don't last forever (while *kindness* keeps you from lashing out unfairly), but that doesn't mean you were necessarily to blame. And when you have all *five* of these elements, being alone, for example, is nothing more than a state of solitude – a numerical fact – instead of a state of mind in which aloneness transforms into loneliness. *Emotional balance* and *self-acceptance* remind you that you don't necessarily *need* to be with someone to feel whole, as *kindness* and goodwill easily keep you connected to the world. *Purpose* and *self-acceptance* tell you that whether alone or with another, you know your place in the world; and, *courage* reminds you that even if you do feel passing twinges of loneliness, you will overcome those feelings in short order. *Courage, emotional balance,* and *kindness* buy you the freedom to be whatever you want; *purpose* allows you to choose what that role and identity happens to be, and *self-acceptance* allows you to be happy with these choices and with yourself. If you have these five, if you follow this formula, there is very little, as you can see, that will have the power to derail your happiness for more than a brief period of time. Learn to like who you are. Do the best you can with what you have and maximize your potential. If you *don't* like who you are, become the best *you* possible until you do.

How noble and good everyone could be, if every evening before falling asleep, they were to recall to their minds the events of the whole day and consider exactly what has been good and bad. Then without realizing it, you try to improve yourself at the start of each new day.[16]

– Anne Frank

The remaining chapters of this book are varied, but all are intended to promote happiness, to reveal pathways for finding it, or to discuss ways to precipitate it in yourself and in others. As you read them, please keep in mind the five foundational elements of *purpose, courage, emotional balance, kindness & other ethics*, and *self-acceptance*, as all of these principles serve as predication and context for the rest that I have written.

Purpose, courage, emotional balance, kindness & ethics, and *self-acceptance*: Master these, and true and thorough happiness will be yours and yours to keep.

Chapter 7

Self-Awareness

Self-awareness is an odd thing, a *Catch-22* type thing: It tends to be valued mostly by those who already have it, but to those that need it most, it is unfortunately rarely even a passing thought. Self-awareness is a very important attribute for an individual to have, *any* individual – *all* individuals. That said, my audience for this chapter, my *particularly* interested audience, that is, will likely be 1) those who are already relatively self-aware and who want to improve their level of self-awareness and 2) those who are not quite sure if they are self-aware or not. As with many things, one can improve one's quotient of self-awareness with a little effort.

Let's first define terms. Self-awareness is one's ability to *realistically* perceive the way in which one thinks and feels and believes about various aspects of themselves. It is also the knowledge or understanding that one has about one's reasons for doing, thinking, and being *X, Y,* and *Z.* It is also an understanding of how one "presents" or appears to others.

Sometimes I talk to people who have complaints about their work performance reviews, their supervisors, or about a colleague or some other relationship. Usually, these conversations go very well. Sometimes, though, there is a discrepancy between what the person believes or *purports* to believe about themselves and what appears *to me* to be more realistically accurate. Part of my job is to discuss this discrepancy and help them to come to a more realistic view of things. The pattern that I routinely observe in these same individuals is that because they are generally good-hearted people, they have a very difficult time admitting they might not be a very good employee, or friend, or whatever the relationship might be. Of course, there is a big difference between *admitting* what you know to be true and actually *believing* it. This is where self-awareness comes in.

Until you make the unconscious conscious, it will direct your life and you will call it fate.[17]

– Carl Jung

There are two primary reasons people may *say* they are exceptional employees, friends, or spouses, for example, when they really don't believe that to be true: denial and pride. But, when a person truly *does* believe they are exceptional – when in fact, by consensus, they are not – this is a case in which self-awareness is the attribute that is lacking.

Self-awareness is a form of emotional intelligence. It is also, at times, a function of honesty and humility. Sometimes, the lack of self-awareness is an innocent obliviousness, and sometimes one's sense of self is simply more wishful than rational. And then there are *extreme* cases when the lack of self-awareness seems almost delusional.

We've all known a few people over the years that thought they were brilliant, when in fact, they were of about average intelligence. We've all known a few people that thought they were the funniest person in the room when no one else thought that but them. And, we've also known people that were upset each time no one in the room chose to go along with their ideas even though they were *certain* their ideas were the best of all the ones discussed. *All* of these people lacked self-awareness to one degree or another – and it hurt them. Because they did not have a realistic perception of themselves, they tended not to be very well thought of, they were not given much respect, they tended to mature more slowly than other people, and, sometimes, there was almost no maturation over time at all.

Self-awareness is what allows a person to *perceptively* self-critique. Those that have the motivation to do so typically evolve *more* and *faster* than those who do not. It is impossible to improve one's self if no revisions are ever made, and to make the necessary revisions, one must first be able to see where revisions are needed. Self-awareness, regardless of the individual, is about the ability to be objective, and objectivity can be difficult to achieve when we are working on ourselves.

Although I am generally considered to be a good editor and proofreader, I am not the best editor/proofreader of my *own* material. Very few, if any, ever are. Reviewing one's own work just doesn't work very well. When I have been working on some written material for several days, I can proofread it "thoroughly" and see no mistakes in it at all, but when I give it to a colleague, they can find several errors in it with very little effort. Self-awareness is very much the same. We can have a lot of it, but we aren't going to see *everything*. When we try to look at ourselves with an objective eye, it's difficult to get it *completely* right, because over time, we get locked into an unintentionally biased view and become deceived by our own blind spots, becoming blind to our own *personal typos*, as it were. It's just one of the many natural susceptibilities of the human mind.

If you are fortunate enough to possess a high quotient of self-awareness, then you are way ahead of the game. But even though your self-assessment abilities may be very good and your objectivity quotient may be very high as well, the best way to ensure that your self-perception and the perception others have of you is congruent is to ask someone to be your "proofreader." You think you're an awesome dancer? Ask a sibling (or an ex-girlfriend). They'll tell it straight. It's possible, just *possible*, you may not be as smooth as you think. You perceive yourself to be an exceptional employee? Ask a co-worker who has no reason to fib (or a former supervisor). You think you're a good public speaker? Hand out feedback forms to your audiences and find out if you're as polished as you think you are. Think you're a good husband, a good coach, a good hockey player? Ask someone for a critique. This only works, of course, if your proofreaders care more about the truth (and *you* in the long-run) than about your potentially hurt feelings in the short-term. Yes, these reckonings can be humbling experiences, but they can also be very enlightening, and enlightenment, no matter what realm we are talking about, can only make us better, *which is the whole point.*

Self-awareness is very often the difference between successfully progressing from "adequate" to "excellent," so if you were not gifted with innate self-awareness, the best way to get there is to find someone who will be a frank and honest assessor of your life-skills. Find someone you trust to be fair and direct and ask them to critique the areas you want to work on. Of course, seeing a counselor, depending on the nature of the discussion, is also an excellent medium for working on various aspects of one's life. But, whichever forum or person you may choose, if you happen to be as well-grounded as you think, they will undoubtedly confirm it. But, if you need a revision or two, they will help shine the light on the things you need to improve.

Chapter 8

Objectivity

Objectivity is an elusive thing. It's elusive mostly because humans are inclined to put emotions before logic in many instances, and emotions tend to blur our vision. Objectivity is about seeking to view things as they truly are, impartially and neutrally. It's a great concept, and it has such valuable application in our daily lives in so many areas. Just think, for instance, how many fewer misunderstandings, frustrations, hurt feelings, anxieties, and fears there would be if everyone tried to be more objective. Objectivity can make your life easier. It can also make your relationships more successful and your every-day perspectives clearer and more informed. Objectivity is a very powerful thing, and a thing I consider a core virtue, albeit a less traditional one.

I like to think of objectivity as the focusing ring on a camera lens or a telescope – the more objectivity we apply, the clearer we see things, and the clearer we see things, the more fairness we can impart in our opinions and in our decisions. Fairness is closely related to logic and logic is closely related to objectivity, but objectivity, sadly, is a virtue that is often underrated and even overlooked. It has integrity, it is pure, it is diligent, and it maintains its purity by keeping logic in focus and emotions at bay. We all demand fairness – it's a very common topic of conversation – but far less common are discussions of objectivity, which I find odd, because fairness and objectivity go hand in hand.

Although it does not seem to be done very commonly by the average individual, it is quite possible to listen to an argument or a story or to ponder a situation and interpret the elements of that situation in a manner that affords a clear understanding of things, if you mindfully commit yourself to objectivity. Most people tend to listen with their emotions, with personal biases, and with an egocentric perspective. An objective listener, however, strips away personal feelings, preferences, and prejudices, and focuses on the facts and listens with their mind.

One of the things I ask people routinely when they tell me that they feel/think a particular thing (when the origins are not immediately clear) is, "What do you base that feeling on?" Or, "What specifically leads you to feel/think that way?" Often what I will hear in return is "Well, I just feel that…" To which I say, "I know, and I am sympathetic, but I am trying to get to the heart of *why* you feel that way." My point, of course, is that in order to draw conclusions, to react to something appropriately, or to have valid and rational reactions to a particular circumstance, it is important that we *do*, *think*, and *feel* with the support of logic and facts. I'll give you an example.

Recently, I was speaking to someone who felt that a project they had submitted to their supervisor must not have been very good because the supervisor had not responded for two days but who had always been very quick to respond in the past. I asked the person if there were any other factors besides the lack of a response that was causing them to fret. "Was your work sub-standard?" "Did you turn it in late?" "Is your boss possibly upset with you about something else?" "Are you leaving out any details that might factor into an explanation?" The answer to all of these was "No." So, my response was this: "Then, why would you not choose to assume that he just hasn't gotten to the e-mail yet, or considered it a lesser priority than some other things that suddenly popped up for him, or that he *loved* your work and was going to respond when he had more time to deliver a more thorough review?" The person paused a while and said, "I just don't think that's what's going on." To which I said gently, "So you have decided, even though there are numerous neutral explanations and even some positive ones, that his lack of response is due to something negative?" *Silence*. "What it seems you have done here," I said, "and what the vast majority of people do in these situations is allow emotions to replace logic in the decision-making process." This is an example of "catastrophizing," a sadly common reaction to anxiety, involving the tendency to impute a worst-case scenario to a routine circumstance. Unfortunately, however, emotions are not very good elements in the process of analysis.

Incidentally, the supervisor in this instance had simply missed the e-mail. He proactively wrote a very nice email in reply to the person apologizing for his late response and complimented the person on their work. *All that worry for nothing.* And all because emotions were inserted where logic and objectivity should have been.

Yes, of course, emotions are appropriate in matters in which emotions are innately part of the decision-making process (i.e., love, compassion, forgiveness, and so on), but in matters where facts are important, emotions generally muddle our minds, steal from our reason, and betray our logic – all in opposition to objectivity. But I want to be very clear here: This is not a wholesale criticism of emotions. I am simply saying that emotions have their place, but we should not allow them to infiltrate all situations.

Objectivity does not factor in biases, personal agendas, or personal insecurities. It does the very opposite. Objectivity sees the world, conversations, behaviors, etc. with an eye towards what can be observed from *numerous* angles (instead of just one), what a fact is, and what can be determined through investigation to be true. You know the best way to know what someone is thinking? *Ask.* It makes no sense to assume, suppose, guess at, or *attribute* motives or thoughts to someone when all you have to do is ask. Besides being very much like a focusing ring on a camera, an arbiter of relationships, an intellectual filter made for reducing anxieties and misunderstandings, objectivity is also an important courtesy and, in my opinion, an *obligation.*

> *Dispassionate objectivity is itself a passion,*
> *for the real and for the truth.*[18]
> – Abraham Maslow

When I was in graduate school studying to be a counselor many years ago, one of the principles we were taught was that of listening to people with an objective mind, learning to discipline ourselves to remove personal feelings and personal biases from the process of elicitation, exploration, and analysis. It was a concept I committed myself to immediately and one that I have earnestly dedicated myself to from that time forward because it was clear to me that objectivity was central to the principles in a counselor's set of values and practices. But one certainly need not be a counselor or any other sort of professional to benefit from and to *bestow* the benefits of objectivity.

I think of objectivity every day. I truly do. I think of it in every meeting, in every conversation, and in every observation. I do this because I believe that objectivity is good all the time and for every person, regardless of one's position or role at home, at work, or in the world. Yes, it is obviously imperative for counselors to be objective, but it is also just as important for teachers, parents, mechanics, investigators, leaders, coaches, judges – people of *any* occupation or walk of life – to be objective. It is a concept that makes everything more fair, more logical, more *actual*, and more in focus, and it is as beneficial to you as it is to others. In my estimation, it is in the same league as kindness. The kinder we are, the better we tend to be treated. Objectivity reciprocates in much the same way. As with kindness, objectivity is inherently good. And what is inherently good should be applied liberally. Give it a try. Make objectivity a central part of your thinking and see if it doesn't pay dividends in your life as well as in the lives of those around you.

Chapter 9

Communication

The importance of communication in any relationship cannot be overstated. At home, at work, with subordinates, managers, children, spouses, neighbors, the public, strangers, etc., there are few things more important than the way we convey our thoughts to another person. And no matter what the environment or subculture, there are a few aspects of communication that are universally important. The following aspects are the ones that I have found to be the most essential in all forms of communication and are the ones that often make the difference between a bad relationship and a good one, or a good one and a great one.

Transparency: Make it clear to the other person *what* you are trying to convey and *why*. Sometimes – many times, actually – we assume for one reason or the other that the person already understands what we are trying to say or "where we are coming from." However, for many reasons, this is often not the case. Transparency is about making it clear as to *what* you are saying and *why* you are saying it. Try to remind yourself at the outset of a conversation that unless it is patently obvious, it can't hurt to state your *whats* and *whys*.

Clarification: When you are finished speaking or writing, check to make sure what you *think* you have conveyed has actually been conveyed. All it takes is a question or two. Many people *think* they are good communicators because of what they hear in their mind. However, what they hear internally and what is actually presented are often two very different things.

Many, *many* a misunderstanding has occurred not because of a disagreement in philosophy but because of *an assumption*. This has happened to me many times, and I have seen it happen to others many times because one or the other party – again, for various reasons – chose to *assume* some intent from a word or phrase instead of simply asking for clarification. Whether clarification is initiated by the speaker or the listener is less important than simply getting the job done correctly. That said, however, as the speaker, I believe that clarifying questions should be routine. For example, *"I'm not looking for agreement necessarily, but have I explained myself well enough?"* or *"I do not want to assume I have been clear – please tell me if more context/details would be helpful…"*

Honesty: Many miscommunications occur because one or the other party is simply not being honest. I'm not talking about an outright lie. I'm talking about the more common "fibs" that people tell each other in conversation because they don't want to be, for example, "confrontational"; they don't want to slow down the conversation; they don't want to seem disagreeable; they don't want to sound "dumb"; or, for any number of other poor excuses, they choose not to be candid. Though these fibs are common and perhaps are in some ways minor, they undermine the conversation in the very same way that false facts undermine any form of an investigation, for example. If I react to a conversational fib, I am unknowingly feeding the conversation with more false information, such that the results of the conversation (just as with an investigation) are suspect because false information leads to *more* false information and, ultimately, to false conclusions. If you care enough to have the conversation and if you care about the person you are speaking to, you should take care to be truthful about the information you are trying to convey, whether that information is first-party subject matter, or a second-party response to that information.

Sometimes, frank conversations can be rather uncomfortable in their honesty, but I have never walked away from a frank conversation and felt as though I didn't know exactly where I stood and what the other person was all about. I cannot say the same about those many conversations I have had in which I felt that what was being told to me was not entirely forthcoming, precise, or complete. For me, there is far more value in an honest conversation than in one that skimps on honesty in the name of "courtesy," "politeness," or self-protection.

Debate: I do not like to *argue*. I say this for several reasons, one of which is that people that are prone to debate things are often accused of being "argumentative." In this vein, one of the most common defenses in a debate or argument is that when one party is at a loss for a sound position, they will often assert, "Oh, you just like to argue," when really, they have no other logical or relevant response. I *despise* argument. *Despise* it. But when I choose to *debate*, I debate either to 1) persuade for the greater good or 2) to better understand the other person's perspective. I do not do so for *the sake* of debate (that's often just *arguing* in my book – no pun intended), and I do not debate to win.

If I believe wholeheartedly in my opinion on a matter, I will often try to persuade others that it is a sound opinion for the benefit of those involved. I like to help people by nature, so providing an opinion or perspective that I believe I can support and defend seems like a good thing to do, especially if it is a subject that is important. But the other reason I will debate an issue is that I like to hear the other person's perspective because I like to expand the breadth of things I can learn. Debate has the ability to penetrate the other person's position in a logical and enlightening way. An *argument,* conversely, rarely leads to a benefit *or* a better understanding.

When a person is "argumentative," he or she is prone to argue the opposite opinion just for the sake of doing so. Argumentative people also seem to enjoy the fight. People that enjoy *debate*, conversely, tend to take an intellectual approach to a discussion with opposing views in a way that tests either the soundness of the other person's perspective or their own. I enjoy debating with someone who feels the same. I like to learn and I like to be around others that like to learn. Argument tends to be angry, and anger isn't pleasant for anyone. So, when you find yourself in a difference of opinion, ask yourself if you really just want to win, or if you truly want to better understand. It will make the difference in your intent and tone, which will make the difference in whether the discussion is an argument or a debate.

Trust: One of the things that is paramount in any well-intentioned debate is trust. If one or both parties do not trust the other, then an honest debate will simply not occur. This is also true of routine conversations, but it is even more pronounced in debate.

If two people trust each other, communication requires little effort. It can feel almost automatic. Messaging is exchanged quickly and efficiently and there is an easy understanding between the two. When trust is lacking, communication is often strained at every juncture.

In talking about trust in communication, what I am talking about is trust with regard to one's motives. When we are talking with someone – debating with them, perhaps – we perceive them as trustworthy or not, and what we are assessing is whether or not what they are saying is true, whether or not they *believe* what they are saying, and what their motive is for saying it. When *any* of these things are suspect, there really can't be any meaningful communication. In fact, this type of conversation is not real communication at all – it is all parry and counter, all strategy, all adversarial (even when polite). It is all gamesmanship and no substance and no sincerity. Without trust (get ready: I'm about to switch from the sword-play analogy to a farming one), this type of conversation is nothing more than an exchange of words that must be winnowed for genuineness by both sides of a suspicious thresher. In the end, both sides draw the same conclusion: *He may be sincere, but I really don't know for sure.* For real and genuine communication to occur, there absolutely must be mutual trust, and if there isn't, there are only two logical options: work to establish trust, or forego the conversation. *Generally* speaking, I see no point in attempting to communicate with someone I do not trust. There are exceptions, of course, but by and large, *meaningful* communication occurs only between parties that have a common trust.

Over-communication: Over-communication, by my definition, has several facets: 1) clarification (thoroughness and precision); 2) includes everything I *am* saying; 3) includes those things I am *not* saying; 4) includes a thorough explanation of context; and 5) has complete transparency. I can't remember exactly when I realized that over-communication was such an important thing, but I can tell you that when I did realize it, I became committed to the philosophy because of its many, many intrinsic benefits, and I have been advocating for it ever since.

As we all know and have often learned the hard way, context is *everything*. Almost always, the more context that is added to an explanation, the better the explanation. Take this scenario, for example:

A parent tells an 8th grade daughter that she should consider focusing as much on English as she does on math. Because the daughter is obedient and humble and loving, she simply nods in agreement and begins spending more time on writing and grammar. What the daughter is thinking but doesn't say, however, is, *"I wonder why they don't think math is important?" "I wonder if it's because girls are supposed to be good at English, and I'm a little better at math?" "I wonder if I should stop spending time on math until I catch up on English?"*

Of course, the parent doesn't think *any* of these things. In fact, the parent *likes* that the daughter is good at math, is proud that the daughter doesn't fall into a false stereotype of girls not being as good at math, and just wants the daughter to be equally good at writing *and* grammar because the parent wants the daughter to be well-rounded and good at *all* subjects. The parent also believes that it makes more sense to spend more time on a subject that the daughter has less natural ability in than on a subject that comes so easily.

"Over-communication" (which, frankly, is just *good* and *thorough* communication), would have had the parent saying this instead: "Because we want you to be excellent in all subjects, we think it is important for you to spend more time studying English. We're *not* saying we want you to spend less time on math. We simply want you to spend more time practicing grammar and writing. We are glad you like math, and we understand that you may have less of an aptitude for English at the moment, but we want you to make 'As' in all subjects, not just the ones you are naturally good at so that you can have more choices when it comes time for college. Even though English is a bit harder for you now, we know that you are smart enough to be just as good at it as you are at math, with a little effort." *Context, precision, thoroughness, transparency*. All of these make for a more meaningful, helpful, and informative conversation.

<u>Listening</u>: If you sincerely want to be a good communicator, you must first be a good listener. It is impossible to respond to someone well, if you have not truly been listening to what they are saying.

Good listening is composed of several things. Most important to the act of listening is making a focused effort to understand what the other person is saying and why they are saying it. Just as these two things are important to you as the speaker, they are also important to you as the listener. If the speaker is conveying the *whats* and *whys* and the listener is doing the same, an effective swatch of communication is very likely to result.

Being a good listener is not an art or even a skill. It is a *decision*. Good listeners *choose* to be good listeners. They choose to listen to each word, to listen to what is said and to those things that are *not* said. At the heart of good listening is caring. If you are not the best listener, all you have to do is decide to care a little more about what is being said, and if you can't be genuinely interested in the content, then do your best to be interested in the speaker – as a person.

Communication works for those who work at it.[19]
– John Powell

One of the things that often impedes our ability to listen is our eagerness to speak. Good listeners are focused on the *speaker*, trying to really absorb what is being spoken. Poor listeners are often just waiting for the speaker to finish, hovering themselves in mid-air, mentally so that they can swoop in and take their turn in the conversation the instant the other party comes to the end of a sentence. If you are composing your thoughts and readying your speaking part while the other person is speaking, you cannot be listening – your ears may be hearing, but your mind is not assimilating. And, of course, especially these days, if you are looking at your phone, or even just thinking about the fact that you may get a call or text, you are not truly focused on the person in front of you.

You cannot truly listen to anyone and
do anything else at the same time.[20]

– M. Scott Peck

We learn to speak at a very early age. It is innate. And because it is innate, we tend to take it (speaking) for granted. But speaking and communication are very different. Speaking comes natural to all of us. It's easy and second-nature. And we may presume that good communication comes natural as well, but it really doesn't. Good communication isn't just talking. It's listening and exchanging, and understanding. Good communication is satisfying and bonding. Poor communication is wasteful and often off-putting, and each speaker determines which of these two ways it goes. If you want to be a better communicator, ensure that you are a good listener and treat communication as a living structure that is built with language, inflection, rhythm, focus, humanity, respect, courtesy, sincerity, humility, and a desire to understand the other person better. If you do this, you will be well respected, well-liked, and well… *happy.*

Chapter 10

Romantic Relationships

Relationships, of the romantic sort, are such a central part of the human experience. Thousands of books have been written on the topic because it *is* so central to whom we are as people. But, for purposes of this chapter, I would like to discuss just one aspect of relationships: an aspect that can easily be argued to be the most critical aspect of all – that of *choosing* the person we want to be in a *romantic* relationship with. If you are already in a sound and permanent relationship, this will not be of much benefit to you, personally. However, it might be of use to you in your role as a Mom/Dad, Aunt/Uncle, Brother/Sister, or Friend.

The two constructs I always focus on when discussing this topic with family, friends, and co-workers are *compatibility* and *chemistry*. These two concepts are not new to anyone, and I seriously doubt I am turning over any new ground on the subject. However, I am confident in saying that these two concepts are all one needs to think about when choosing a potential partner. Anything outside of these two is simply not integral to the decision, in my estimation. But, before I go further in this discussion, it is important, as always, to define terms.

Chemistry, to me, is innate physical attraction, *plus*. It is physical attraction that goes, almost literally, to the molecular level. Chemistry is attraction that causes a person to be "in love" with just about everything the other person transmits to the five senses. Just having an intense physical attraction for someone is not real chemistry, at least not as I choose to define it. Chemistry is, well… *chemistry*. It's how the taste of apple pie melds so well with the taste of ice cream, or how a certain perfume smells pretty good on one woman but *perfect* on another. It's how beige and brown complement each other and how red and yellow really don't. Chemistry in humans is almost visible. In fact, I would argue that it *is* visible in that many of us would claim to be able to "see" when two people are truly meant for each other.

On the other side of things is compatibility. As with chemistry, I apply a very stringent definition, a higher standard to the definition of compatibility than is perhaps employed by others. I see compatibility as how well-matched two people are in relation to how they address the world, how they navigate *in* the world, *not*, for instance, in whether both people like the same sports team or the same types of food. I measure compatibility by the important things: ethics, morals, standards of behavior, philosophical beliefs – you know, the *big* stuff. Many times, however, we are told by friends and loved ones that liking the same music, the same teams, the same places to vacation, the same TV shows, and the like, are important and that the big stuff can be worked out later. I could not disagree more.

TV shows are not who we are – *beliefs* are. The beach or the mountains do not define us. But our ethics do. It's always nice to enjoy watching the same show together, but if the other person doesn't want to watch re-runs of *Gunsmoke* with me, I understand that and do not then perceive this lack of desire as an aspect of incompatibility (although it does make me wonder why someone wouldn't want to watch *Gunsmoke*). What I *do* find incompatible, though, is trying to form a relationship with someone that, for example, doesn't feel compelled to give to the less fortunate or who isn't polite to the waiter/waitress, if the other person *does* feel compelled to do these things. These things are far more defining of a person in that they define *attributes* (in this example, *charity* and *kindness*). Sure, both liking to go to a sports bar may make for a fun date, but the majority of lasting relationships do not sustain themselves on this type of compatibility. Think of it this way: Are you going to be able to have love, affection, and respect for someone that is dismissive of or disinterested in animals, if you are a person who feels led to take care of animals? Are you going to be okay with someone who lives check-to-check when you are someone who believes in always having a savings account *and* a solid cushion in your checking account? Do you really think that the person you want to commit to, with whom you have many hobbies and interests in common, isn't going to lose their charm once you realize that they believe that "life sort of just happens the way it happens," while you are a staunch believer in personal responsibility? These *big things* are the types of compatibility that matter. The other stuff just doesn't – not ultimately. Like-mindedness is not about low-level preferences. It is about direction and meaning in living life, not ice cream toppings, and favorite colors.

"But don't opposites attract?" I am routinely asked. Well, yes, sometimes. "Opposites" tends to imply, for example, introverted vs. extroverted, easy-going vs. frenetic, or vigilant vs. care-free. Sometimes, they are a disastrous combination and sometimes they are an excellent one. Now, guess what tends to make the difference in which of these occurs? That is correct: *Chemistry*. Which leads perfectly to my next point and the answer to the question you may not have known you had: *"So, which is more important, chemistry or compatibility?"*

Never, ever should a person feel compelled for any reason to choose one of these over the other. *Both* are extremely important. Both are *crucial*. But, answering this question for the sake of pure curiosity actually helps me make my point about the importance of *chemistry*, which, to answer the question, is the *slightly* more important of the two.

Chemistry, which manifests itself most particularly in physical attraction, has the mysterious ability to enhance understanding, heighten cooperation, preempt and mitigate disagreements, to incite forgiveness, and to kindle synergy. If you absolutely have to put one slightly higher than the other, *go with chemistry.*

In the many years I have been discussing the topic of relationships with people, I have found that beyond the mistake of not looking for people with whom they have chemistry *and* compatibility, they also tend to make this other major mistake when beginning a relationship: *They compromise their standards.*

In talking to a co-worker, a close friend, or even just an acquaintance about this very common topic of conversation, I will advise them, in the context of a new relationship, to make a list of attributes they are looking for in a significant other. I ask them to include in this list only those *must-haves* and *will-not-accepts.* Ninety-nine percent of the time, the final list is perfectly reasonable and even well-considered. But, in *revisiting* the list with them after a few weeks or months of dating their potential candidate, I very frequently find that the list-maker has scratched off one or more items in each of the two categories in order to accommodate those things the *latest* significant-other candidate is lacking. I would estimate this happens at least eight out of ten times I conduct this exercise. When I ask why the person decided to scrap a *must-have* or *will-not-accept*, the person almost always says they think they were being too critical (even though in the initial formation of the list, the person was confident in their itemized requirements). When I say to the person that I do not think any of the items were too critical (or I would have stated so initially), I also tell them that I think they have altered their standards based on one or more factors, and then I present to them a list of factors I think might have influenced their changes. Forthcoming people will eventually tell me that they did, in fact, revise their standards for one or more of the items below as reasons for their compromise:

- Financial concerns
- Boredom/loneliness
- Companionship/sex
- Social expiration (worry about aging out of the "market")
- Fear of being lonely later in life

There are several others, but these are the most common.

Recently, I was speaking to a female friend of mine about this very subject. She commented that the guy she had just gone out with was very kind, smart, etc., and that he "checked some boxes, but didn't really ring any bells." I asked her why then she was considering another date with him, and she said because she wasn't sure that she really had "any other options," (implying that whatever guy has asked her out at the time is her only option). I told her that while I understood how she felt and sincerely sympathized, I was concerned about her perspective given that I don't believe that anyone should "settle" (compromise one's standards and settle for less than is hoped for).

Let me say here that I understand that women reading this might say to themselves, *"Well, that's easy for you to say – you're a man,"* and I do understand that reaction. But, because I cared about this person, my duty as a caring friend was to provide the best wisdom possible, and wisdom tells me that no matter how many "reasons" there may be for wanting to settle, settling is never a wise choice. I have met and know many people that have settled. *Many*. And, while some of these people are *relatively* content, the great majority are not. I often say to people that the only thing worse than being unhappy and alone is being unhappy and living in the same house with someone you do not love. Loneliness is bad, but loneliness when you are not actually alone is even worse.

Settling will sometimes solve the initial problem (financial concerns, loneliness, whatever the case may be), but as with so many other examples of short-term solutions, the *long-term* effects of settling are many and dire. Those that settle tend to be resentful, aggravated, angry, a poor significant other, dreadful, sad, depressed, and just generally unhappy. And don't forget that when a person settles, they also effectively take themselves off the market, taking away the best option for finding love, *which is finding a better match*.

"But what of love itself," you ask?

Many of you might have noticed, and are scratching your head even now, perhaps, that I did not discuss "love," *per se*, very much at all in this chapter, even though it is a chapter on romance and loving relationships (in fact, I have used the word "love" only five times prior to this sentence). These are my reasons: Love is intuitive to most everyone. I couldn't imagine that any of you would find value in listening to me wax on about what *I* think it is or how *I* think it relates to happiness. In my mind, a discussion of love is implied in a discussion of "romantic relationships," so I tried to spare you the parts that felt obvious. Secondly, love is different things to different people and I did not want to presume to say that what it is to me is what it is or should be to others. Third, a discussion of love could take up thousands of pages, and *has* taken up tens of thousands of pages already elsewhere. I did not think I could do justice to the topic, and it was just not part of my objective to include it. Fourth, though many would argue that love

59

is required for a person to be happy, there will be many that disagree. Yes, the numbers in these two camps will be quite different – perhaps 10:1 or even 100 or 1000:1 – but in any case, there will be many who say that happiness does not require love, so I did not include it in the formulaic elements I believe to be essential. Is it, as Tennyson proclaimed, *"...better to have loved and lost than never to have loved at all"*? [21] Most might agree, but some would not…

Lastly on the topic of love itself, all I know for sure is this: *Love is powerful.* As powerful as anything I have written about in this book. In fact, if there is anything *more* powerful in the cosmos of humanity, I am not familiar with it.

I know many people believe in this next cliché, but I am not aware of any credible information or belief system that compels *me* to believe that there is *one "right person" for everyone.* I have always believed that a person could fall in love with any number of people, if everything fell into place just right. In fact, I believe that there could easily be 10 or even 20 people that one *could* encounter in a lifetime that may meet all of one's requirements for chemistry and compatibility. If I am right, settling doesn't seem like a very prudent (or necessary) thing to do. I have no examples of someone I know that settled *and* was happy, but I have *many* examples of friends and acquaintances who settled who are *not.*

> *Choose your life's mate carefully. From this one decision will come 90% of all your happiness or misery.* [22]
> – H. Jackson Brown

For those of you about to enter into a new relationship, make your list (*must-haves/will-not-accepts*). Be fair and reasonable and list all those things that you require in a significant other in order to feel both chemistry and compatibility and all those things that are deal-breakers. Then, all you have to do is stay true to your list. Miss or Mister Right sometimes falls into our laps, but it doesn't happen very often, so you have to work a little. Make yourself available, let your friends know you are available, make *them* aware of your list, and tell them not to send anyone your way that isn't fully up to specs. Think about it: How many story-book endings have you heard that start with *"Well, you see, it all started when I settled…"?*

Chapter 11

Passive-Aggressive Behavior

Passive-aggressive behavior, very simply, is *aggressive* behavior displayed in a *passive* way. For example, a significant other might choose to express their lack of forgiveness after an argument by refusing to eat the meal their partner prepared for them, even though it was that significant other's favorite meal. Instead of transparently and assertively telling the person they were not yet over the argument, the significant other *passive-aggressively* sends this message by not eating a meal that they otherwise would have welcomed and enjoyed. Not saying "good morning," intentionally not replying to texts until hours after receiving them, claiming to "forget" important dates or facts, arriving late, avoiding eye contact, and taking issue with someone over things that don't seem relevant or important, are often examples of passive-aggressive behavior. Another way of putting it is *aggressive* behavior perpetrated in a sneaky, dishonest, and/or indirect way.

> *Passive-aggression – Being covertly spiteful with the intent of inflicting mental pain.*[23]
> – Ashta Chaitanya [Ashta-deb]

Passive-aggressive behavior can originate in a number of ways, but people often develop this negative way of dealing with conflict because they learned it from someone close to them, either by simple observation or, in some respects, by passive instruction. Many of you might be frowning as you read that, but it's true. Many times, one parent or the other teaches their child that they should not be rude or confrontational so that they will not appear as "trouble-makers," and instead choose to walk away and be perceived as "nice," even when the other person initiated the conflict. Children, especially girls in our American culture (and, undoubtedly, in some others), are often taught that confrontation and argument are not "lady-like" and that they need to stifle their negative reactions to interpersonal conflicts. The problem with this, of course, is that while one might be able to stifle one's reactions to the *external* conflict, it is very difficult to suppress the *internal* conflicts that occur because one felt obligated not to say anything about whatever injustice had taken place.

It is only natural for us to dislike and resent not "having our say," especially when we feel wronged. The problem then becomes *where* this resentment goes, and we all know it doesn't just go away – which is often how passive-aggressive behavior begins. Passive-aggressiveness almost always has animosity attached to it. Whether it's from anger, resentment, frustration, or some other specific form of hostility, animosity is central to why one chooses the *aggressive* half of the term. The *passive* half is another matter.

The passive aspect of passive-aggressiveness, as discussed, can be a learned behavior, or it can be a simple lack of courage. Many times, people will say things like, *"Oh, it just wasn't worth fighting about,"* or *"I was just as much at fault,"* or *"Oh, it doesn't bother me,"* when, in fact, none of these statements are representative of the person's true feelings. So, if this is not how we feel, why do say these things? *Because we are afraid.* We are afraid of the conflict (of the confrontation itself and the anxiety we feel as it is occurring), we are afraid of feeling "bested" because we are not adept at defending ourselves, we are afraid because we are concerned that things could escalate, we are afraid of drawing attention to ourselves, we are often afraid of "becoming emotional," and we are afraid of unknown outcomes. What we perceive the *passive* in passive-aggressiveness does is allow us to put things back in our own control. When we choose this option, it is often because we get to name the time and place of these passive-aggressions, which allows us to avoid the perils of a conventional confrontation. Of course, these calculations regarding control are undoubtedly subconscious, but they are no less actual.

So how does a person decide to stop being passive-aggressive? The first thing one must do is decide that an assertive, more courageous, more in-command-of-one's-self is a better way of life than the one they are living.

Becoming assertive is theoretically very easy. What makes it difficult, in practice, is making it a habit and a new way of life. But this is all that is required:

- Tell people how you feel
- Tell people how you feel *as soon as you feel it*. [Now, it is okay and even advisable to temper things and to deliver your thoughts in a measured way. I am not suggesting that you must necessarily present your thoughts in their rawest form. A bit of filtering is often helpful and even wise]
- Commit to the philosophy every day and in every conversation

You will naturally feel anxiety at first – the same as with anything that you are trying out for the first time – but if you do it consistently, calmly, and with forethought, it will get easier and easier each time. I guarantee it. [Please see written guarantee at the end of this book.]

In the many years that I have been discussing this subject with people, I can tell you that I have seen very few "converts." And although the percentage of those that were once passive-aggressive but are not now is relatively low, I can also tell you that not one of them would return to their old way of life under any circumstances. Passive-aggressive behavior is not *just* a behavior. In fact, more often than not, it is a way of life. If courage can be a way of life – and hopefully I have convinced you it can be – then fear, unfortunately, can be as well, and very often *does* become a way of life, and at the heart of most passive-aggressive thinking and behavior *is* fear. And, fear is a prison to which we, and we alone, have the key. [An article I stumbled onto a while back that is very well-written and very insightful is *"Why So Many Women are Passive-Aggressive (and How I Stopped)"* by "Han" at *curiouswriter.com*. Whether you are a man or a woman, I think it would be well worth your time to read it.]

1) Passive aggression is very unhealthy, and my goal in writing this book is to facilitate mental health (= happiness); 2) Passive-aggression undermines and marginalizes whoever employs it, and I genuinely want people – especially women – to feel empowered and equal in a society that is easily argued to be male dominated; 3) I am neither

feminist nor anti-feminist. I am simply a person dedicated to helping others improve their mental health by helping them to improve their self-esteem, their self-image, their self-respect, and their ability to become more comfortable with whom they are. My sincere belief is that helping people to decrease the frequency of passive-aggressive behavior – whether men or women – will make them feel better about themselves and, thus, better about life. That is my objective as I write this now and my objective each day that I come to work, speak to my female friends, talk to my sister, and to my four female nieces (yes, I just said "female nieces." I am trying to make it clear that my female relationships are important to me, but perhaps this grotesque redundancy was quite unnecessary, but, I reckon it's too late now…).

Ladies and gentlemen, if you tend to engage in passive-aggressive behavior, do everything possible to break this habit. I have never known anyone who is passive-aggressive that is truly happy. If you want to be happy, you must learn to be *assertive* instead. It is well worth the effort and will change your life. And that is no exaggeration.

Chapter 12

Procrastination

You know how it seems like your car runs a little better when you have a full tank of gas (no matter how illogical you realize that is)? You know how after you pay a round of monthly bills, you get a little bounce in your step? You know how after you finish writing thank you notes after attending a party, for instance, you feel lighter and slightly more carefree? Well, how would you like to feel that infusion of energy all the time? How would you like to wake up every morning and feel like you don't really have too many worries, after all? Well, my friends, all you have to do is stop procrastinating. Get the stuff done you have been putting off and you will feel better about almost everything.

Life brings with it all sorts of chores and drudgeries: yard work, the dishes, housecleaning, fixing the garage door, putting gas in the car, paying bills, thank you notes, etc. *and etc*. They are unavoidable. But what *is* avoidable is the feeling of dread, lack of energy, and the desire to procrastinate that comes from allowing things to build up *due to procrastination*. Yes, you read that correctly: Desire to procrastinate often comes from the problems that procrastination has already caused. Procrastination leads to more procrastination – and the cycle never ends. Would you like to know the mysterious and age-old solution to ending your habit of procrastination? *Just stop it.*

Let's say you have a mental list of about 15-20 things you have been putting off doing. Most are pretty small, one or two are kind of big, the rest are medium. Because we are all very different when it comes to personal things like this, I won't presume to tell you that there is a proven system of triage that will work for everyone. What I can advise, however, is that starting on your list by choosing *any three* to complete back-to-back *will* give you an immediate sense of accomplishment and will more than likely impel you to do *more* than just three of the things on your list. The point is to *just get started*. But, before you actually get started, put your list in writing. *This is important.*

Spend some time thinking of all the things you need to get done. Make a sincere effort to make the list complete and carry the list with you. I make lists on my phone, but I have found that carrying around a "hard copy" list is sometimes more effective in keeping these chores in the forefront of my mind. Once you have your complete list in hand, pick at least three items to complete, set aside some time on a Friday evening or a Saturday morning (or Tuesday at 9:23 p.m., if that's the sweet spot for you) and get started. As soon as you complete your three tasks, you will feel an immediate sense of hope, accomplishment, and even relaxation. Skeptical? *Try it.* What do you have to lose?

Allowing chore list items to build up, or *any* unfinished business for that matter, causes an accumulation of subconscious dread. The more dread we feel, even when it is subconscious, the more unsettled and preoccupied we feel. Have you ever wondered *why* it feels like the car runs better when the tank is full? It's because having a full tank gives us one less thing to worry about. In fact, it gives us *several* less things to worry about: We won't be running out of gas on the road; we won't have to stop in the heat (or cold) and get our hands dirty; and, we won't be late for work because we first had to stop for gas. The car seems to run better because as soon as we fill the tank, we have taken one thing off our list that was causing us dread. Less dread, more happiness – a "zero-sum formula," as they say.

> *Nothing is so fatiguing as the eternal hanging*
> *on of an uncompleted task.*[24]
>
> – William James

When you have a list of unfinished chores, your time is not your own. Not really – not unfettered, anyway. You owe that list your time – part of your life, as it were – and you drag it around with you wherever you go. The list and all the tasks you have been putting off become part of your subconscious, but the list doesn't go away just because you are avoiding it – no more so than avoiding the ever-growing lawn causes the lawn to mow itself. The subconscious is real and it tends to operate just far enough under the surface to be out of your frame of perception, but not so deep that it misses the opportunity to nag at you throughout the day in passively, but ugly and annoying ways.

Subconscious anxieties caused by unfinished or unresolved matters manifest themselves in our daily lives in many different ways. Sometimes we feel dread; sometimes we feel tired; sometimes we feel distracted or unnerved. More often, we feel a little "touchy," sensitive, more prone to aggravation, or moody. But, just as many of us do with chronic pain, we avoid addressing all these subconscious feelings and learn to live with them on a daily basis, such that these feelings eventually come to feel "normal." And once we choose to accept and label them as normal, we no longer feel compelled to make a change – because why would we need to change something that is "normal"? But, do you know when it is you learn that what you have been feeling is *not* normal? *As soon as you complete the list*, which immediately removes the nagging, preoccupying dread, avoidance, and anxiety that you felt as your list continued to build. The moral? *Nothing* unresolved is good.

When your list is done, *all* of your time is your own, and you can be carefree. Think about it: Wouldn't you like to have a clean slate? Wouldn't you like to wake up on a Saturday and have nothing that you really *need* to get done? Wouldn't you like to have some time in which you can truly decompress, breathe easy, and enjoy life? All it takes is a single moment in time. A split second in which you get up from the couch, set your jaw, and say, *"OK, today's the day I start on my list."*

You want to be happier in life? *Good.* Now all you have to do is *mean* it. And that just requires a little effort. Start on your list and don't stop 'til it's done. Your happiness, sense of accomplishment, and calm will increase immediately. *It works. It works. It works.* I guarantee it. [Please see written guarantee at the end of this book.]

Chapter 13

Anger

Anger affects mental health as much as any emotion. When one is angry, it is impossible to be content, peaceful, or anything *close* to happy.

Anger is very human, very natural, and is very often the appropriate emotion for us to feel, especially in situations in which anger is caused by the unfair or unjust act of someone else. If someone harms a member of our family, we feel angry. If someone rudely cuts us off in traffic, we feel angry. If someone says things about us that are untrue, we feel angry. All of these are perfectly legitimate reasons to feel angry. In these examples, assuming we are reasonable in our reactions, these bursts of anger or periods of *pronounced* anger are relatively short-lived and we move on relatively quickly. Sometimes, though, because of less definitive events or circumstances, we feel anger that is usually less intense but lasts much longer (chronic vs. acute). Often, this type of anger – *chronic* anger – results from unresolved conflict whether within ourselves or with another person. It is *chronic* anger that I will be discussing here.

People can harbor anger for any number of reasons. Financial hardships, relationship difficulties, poor self-image, feeling unlucky and picked on by the world, health problems, and loneliness are some of the more common reasons people feel chronic anger. Regardless of the reason, persistent feelings of anger can seep into all parts of our daily lives and cause us to view the world in a very biased and often distorted way. It can also cause us to behave in ways that are not very positive and in ways that we may not even be aware of. Anger like this can be very similar to chronic pain, and we all know, either from our own experience or from knowing someone else suffering from chronic pain, that it is a very energy-draining and debilitating thing to have to cope with on a daily basis. Anger is very much the emotional equivalent of chronic pain.

Just as with physical pain, anger can make you more impatient than usual. It can make it more difficult to get restful sleep, more difficult to truly focus, and more difficult to maintain a cheerful disposition. Underlying feelings of anger can make one gloomy or negative or "off" from whatever it is to feel normal and without anger. As with chronic pain, the self-perception that you are coping with it well on a daily basis doesn't mean it isn't perceivable by other people. As someone who had chronic pain for many years, I know that while most people did not know I was in pain, those closest to me *were* aware of it, particularly after I was able to get relief from most of it years later. Shortly after I had some good luck with a back surgery some years ago, a good friend of mine said, "Is your back better – you seem like you're in an extra good mood today?" I had always gone out of my way to stifle any signs of being in pain, but clearly, being in pain for many years had caused me to be less happy than I was aware of, even though I coped with it outwardly relatively well.

Anger, like chronic pain, is insidious. It often sneaks up slowly and hangs around quietly without any sudden or startling movements. Many of us are able to manage our reactions to it so that it doesn't reveal itself except to those who are particularly in tune. But, just as with chronic pain, anger takes a toll, and it almost never goes away on its own. So, what do you do if you are angry due to some unresolved conflict? The exact same thing you do when you have chronic pain: Determine the source and commit to resolving it.

> *Anger is an acid that can do more harm to the vessel in which it is stored than to anything on which it is poured.*[25]
>
> *– Mark Twain*

All anger has a source. There is no such thing as *idiopathic* anger. Most of the people I have talked to with "anger issues" eventually reveal what the source of their anger is. Those that don't – rather those that *won't* (because they claim they can't or truly cannot figure it out) – are just not being honest or are extremely un-self-aware. Even people that may have buried the source of their anger for many years have the ability to dig it up. Ninety-nine percent of the time, all it takes is sincere conversation and a little insight, and the source or *sources* of anger can be dug out from the many layers of the sediment of life. In the 1% of instances in which the individual claims not to be able to divine the source of the anger, it always appears to me to be a matter of pride that is preventing them from identifying the source out loud – the person is simply not ready to *admit* the source or isn't ready to *disclose* the source of the anger. But, when the source of the anger *has* been identified, all that's left to do is work on resolution, which is truly not very difficult.

Depending on the individual, resolving anger can take a long time or very little. For those people earnestly committed to getting rid of the anger in their lives, to changing their lives by changing their perspective and/or their circumstances, it doesn't take long at all. But no matter the personality involved or the nature of the anger, the first step to freeing one's self of underlying anger falls into one of two categories, generally speaking: *confrontation* (of the source, psychological or human) and/or *acceptance*.

Sometimes, we are angry about things we cannot change. I knew a man long ago who told me that in his early adulthood he was angry because he was only 5'4." I knew this man to be intelligent, strong, nice-looking, talented, and quick-witted, among other things, but when he was younger, his height bothered him a great deal and he harbored an underlying anger for a large portion of his life, which, by his own admission, led to many years of alcoholism. To tell this story quickly, once he acknowledged the reason for his anger and accepted that his height was something he could not change, he stopped drinking and led a fulfilled life. When I met him in his 50s, he had been in recovery for more than 25 years, and I can tell you without hesitation that I never saw any remnants of his former anger. Acceptance is a switch. All one needs to do is flip it. Acceptance just takes will, and once he decided to have it, to exercise it, his anger went away.

As to the other category of dealing with anger – confronting the origin of it, whether it is an event, or a person, or a condition – I have known many people over the years that carry with them an under-the-surface anger that, in essence, smolders like hot embers that have been covered over with a measure of soil. Every now and then, you will feel a little heat and perhaps see a wisp of smoke, but rarely do you see any flame penetrate to the surface. Anger like this can burn for years, and often does, because the individual has never had the inclination or the courage to try to extinguish it. Once you have discovered the origins of your anger or have simply decided to acknowledge them, all that is left to do is decide if you are willing to address how you got to your present emotional state and resolve the problem.

If you find that you do not have the most cheerful disposition, you are routinely irritable, are prone to aggravation over relatively minor things, feel negative about life in general, or seem to be less happy than others around you, it might be worth asking yourself if your unhappiness is due to unresolved conflict or due to issues that cause you to feel an underlying and persistent anger. Identifying these issues and either accepting them or working to resolve them *does* work. No one should live with chronic anger and no one has to. All it takes to get rid of it, as with most things, is a little effort.

Chapter 14

Decision-Making Made Easy

We make decisions every day. Hundreds of them. *Thousands,* actually. And most of them are made on auto-pilot – that is, we are not deliberating very much when we make them. And that is okay for those decisions that do not really require a lot of deliberation – making lane changes as we drive to work, opening the mail when we get home, taking off our shoes and changing into our evening attire, for example. All of these things are pretty much automatic. But there are many other decisions we make that are far more consequential, and over the years, I have done my best to make it a *habit* to be mindful of the more important decisions I make each day, and in doing so, I arrived at a very simple way of making these decisions in a logical and methodical way.

I start with the notion that all decisions should be made based on a hierarchy of importance, whereby the higher element (Tier) takes precedence over any lower one, with logic/reason running in the background at every juncture. These are the tiers, as I have constructed them:

Tier I.	Morals
Tier II.	Ethics
Tier III.	Laws
Tier IV.	Policies/Guidelines
Tier V.	Cultural Practices/Mores/Customs/Etiquette
Tier VI.	The Preferences of Others
Tier VII.	Personal Preferences

*Logic (safety, health, financial considerations, etc.)

I first ask myself if there are *morals* involved. If there are, I choose the highest moral I can discern and choose in its favor. If no moral exists, I move to *ethics* and repeat the process. I then ask, in the absence of any ethics, if there are *laws* involved. If no laws apply, I move to *policies* and/or *guidelines*. If none exist, I move down to *cultural practices, customs, etiquette*, and the like; then, I move one step lower to the *preference of others*, and lastly to the lowest level of importance – *my own personal preferences*. Naturally, there is often overlap, so I simply defer to the highest element in the order. To better illustrate the concept, I will go through this process with a few examples.

Example 1: A farm-owner friend of mine tells me that several of his chickens have been killed by a neighbor's dogs, both of which dogs are the neighbor's family pets. My friend reminds me that the law allows him to kill the dogs which are in his yard at this moment, that they have come over before and will no doubt come over again. He asks me what I think he should do, and because I know he is genuinely conflicted, I ask him if he can do anything to better deter the neighbor's dogs and/or to fortify the protection for his chickens. He says that he can, so I advise him to go scare the dogs away and to notify the neighbor that the dogs were not shot (even though nine out of 10 farm owners, rightly or wrongly, would have killed the dogs). Based on this hierarchical system, there are at least two moral considerations involved, in my opinion, which operate at a higher level than the law in this example. Those morals are kindness/compassion and forbearance/forgiveness.

Although the law would, in fact, allow my friend to kill the dogs that killed his chickens, the hierarchy as I have devised it, puts morals above the law (although morals and laws very often intersect), such that morals are given greater weight in the decision-making process. *Forgiveness* for the transgression committed by the neighbor's dogs and *kindness* and compassion for their feelings of love for these pets supersede the allowances made by the law. Killing the dogs is a legal right in many, if not most, jurisdictions – authorized and even justified, depending on one's point of view and/or environment. However, a more prudent decision, perhaps, if not a more noble one, is to put aside what is *allowed* and to consider these things:

- What's done is done. Killing the dogs will not resurrect the chickens and does not, cannot make anyone "whole"

- The neighbor's insurance will pay for the replacement cost of the chickens
- Forgiveness, compassion, and forbearance spares the neighbor's family the sorrow of losing their dogs
- Though not owed, forgiveness, compassion, and forbearance breed goodwill between the farmer and his neighbor
- Drastic actions, while sanctioned (if not also justified by one condition or another) often cause more regret than do actions of restraint

Example 2: A supervisor asks what I think he should do with regard to an employee who routinely comes in to work 30 minutes late. Before she became his supervisor, the employee worked in this job role and had been coming in late for many years, though she *is* aware that he does, in fact, work the required eight hours per day by making up the time at the end of the day. I ask the supervisor if she has ever discussed the matter with the employee and she tells me that she has not. I then provide the following assessment based on my decision-making hierarchy.

"In my opinion, until you insist that person come in on time and he fails to comply, there isn't a persuasive reason for you to be upset. He is not doing anything immoral, unethical, or against the law [Tiers I-III] in coming in late, given that you have never counseled him on his arrival time. And, he is also not breaking any policy [Tier IV], even though the normal workday is considered to be 8:00a.m. – 5:00 p.m." I also point out that "the culture [Tier V] at this workplace widely allows for employees to come in to work at many varied times, as long as they are working their full eight hours, which he is doing." I then ask the supervisor if she is bothered that he comes in late because she is concerned about how she is being perceived regarding allowing him to come in late, or if she is simply bothered by the fact that the employee is always 30 minutes late, even though his tardiness is always made up at the end of the workday. She responds that she simply prefers that people arrive "on time." Based on this answer, this was my response to her:

"You have every right to ask that your employees show up by 8:00 a.m. However, in a large city, where traffic is often unpredictable, arriving by 8:00 a.m. might also mean showing up early (in order not to be late), which means, in turn, that employees will naturally expect to be able to *leave* early (earlier than 5:00 p.m.) – the point being that while you may believe that an 8:00 a.m. – 5:00 pm. schedule is ideal, it is also not always practical given the totality of factors that affect when people arrive for work, and in requiring such, you are necessarily agreeing that people can leave early, which prompts this inevitable question: 'Is arriving late really that much worse than leaving early?'" I also point out to her that "people often have good reasons for when they come to work (usually related to family responsibilities) and that discussing *his* reasons might make the difference between whether you still feel compelled to require him to come in at 8:00 a.m. (versus 8:30 a.m.), all of which is easily resolved with a simple conversation."

Example 3: I am traveling, am in a hotel, it's late, but I decide I want a soft drink. I go down the hall to the vending machines and consider my options, as I try to decide whether I want a Coke, a Pepsi, or a Dr. Pepper product.

To my knowledge, no living creatures are harmed by any of these manufacturers, none are any more or less responsible than the other for environmental problems that may exist (I certainly don't know of any), and none of the three, to my knowledge, is associated with any other question of moral turpitude (that covers *Tiers I and II)*. And, in good faith, I can say the same about these three corporations with respect to ethical considerations and legal questions, as well (*Tier III*). And, neither the company I work for nor my health insurance carrier prohibit me from drinking any of these beverages (*Tier IV*), so now I am all the way down the list to *Tier V* at "cultural practices," and none of these three soft drinks are forbidden by any mores, traditions, or social values – within my own set of individual practices, that is. And, because I am not traveling with anyone, there are no one *else's* beverage choices for me to be concerned with (*Tier VI*), so I am left to make a decision based on nothing more than my own personal preference in the given moment

(*Tier VII*). But just before I press the button for one of these, I remember that I really should be cutting down on caffeine, so I buy a bottled water instead – as per the dictates of health considerations, i.e., *logic*.

So, if you're not making decisions based on a similar formula or you are using no formula at all, how *are* you making your decisions?

I can tell you from many years of observation that most people, who use no form of decision-making hierarchy, make decisions when there is more than one direction to choose from, based largely on these influences:

- Selfishness
- Pride, vanity
- Fear, aversion
- Guilt
- Anger
- Impatience, impulsiveness, having the inability to delay gratification
- Insecurity
- Poor logic, lack of information, unreasonableness
- Irresponsibility, lack of ethics
- Self-deceit, lack of self-awareness

None of these are part of any system or formula at all. *Each* of these, when written singly and in black and white, are clearly ill-advised and make for a very poor foundation on which to base any decision, yet, unfortunately, many people – if you could get them to be honest with themselves – would admit that these really are the factors that influence their daily decisions. Let's look at some simple examples of these.

An employee is asked as a subject matter expert to provide an opinion on a subject that he knows will be embraced by almost everyone except for his direct supervisor. He chooses to equivocate, fearing a negative reaction by the supervisor. Whether the fear is warranted or not is not particularly relevant in this context. *Fear over ethics.*

A parent chooses not to discipline an ill-behaved child due to guilt over a recent divorce. *Guilt over responsibility.*

One co-worker (co-worker A) asks another for guidance with regard to a logistical matter, and the other co-worker (co-worker B) says they are too busy at the moment to assist and asks co-worker A to consult with someone else. The truth is that co-worker B does not know how to help but is too embarrassed to admit it. *Pride over honesty.*

A man asks his neighbor if he can borrow an inexpensive tool for a short period of time, and the neighbor tells him he cannot locate the tool, when, in fact, he doesn't want to loan it to the man because the man supports a different political party than he does. *Anger over reasonableness.*

A young woman has texted her friend, who has not responded for several hours. Instead of waiting longer for a response, the woman sends a very lengthy and critical text accusing her friend of being mean and avoiding her – only to find out a short time later that her friend had forgotten her phone and was simply unable to reply. *Insecurity and impatience over logic/objectivity.*

The point of these examples is that *without* guiding principles, the decisions we make can be very impulsive, erratic, and unwise. What we choose to eat for dinner, what color car we buy, or what brand of power tools we prefer, for example, are really not very important in the scheme of things. But when there are people and feelings involved and co-workers and family and friends and the public and any context of human existence that involves our interaction with others, how we make these higher-order decisions *matters.*

> *It is not hard to make decisions when you
> know what your values are.*[26]
>
> – Roy Disney

Chapter 15

Regret

I have had many regrets in my life. Many. The cause of some of my regrets are embarrassing, some make me disappointed in the person I was at that moment in the past, some make me wonder how I was ever able to swim out of the quagmire I got myself into, some make me shrug and shake my head with a grin, and others are simply... *regrettable*. None of them, however, live in the forefront of my mind, none cause me any significant angst, and none keep me from moving forward. I have been able to overcome regret in my life because I learned some years ago that in order to be mentally healthy and happy, it was necessary to put my regrets in perspective, to minimize the damage and maximize their potential, as it were. I hope by the end of this chapter you will be able to put your regrets in the proper perspective, as well, so that you can continue to improve in your own growth and happiness.

People tend to deal with regret in one of three ways: They 1) analyze the cause, address it, and move on; 2) gloss over it, repress it, and *kind of* move on; or, 3) dwell on it and harbor it, instead of attempting to resolve it, never really ever moving past it at all.

Glossing over regret, for example – trying to forget about it – cheats us out of an opportunity to learn from our mistakes. Sure, pondering regretful situations is unpleasant – I don't like it any more than you do – but there isn't anything much better for getting smarter and wiser than taking the time to learn from the opportunities that loss, regret, error, failure, etc. afford us. But, as much as repressing our regrets may be irresponsible, *dwelling* on them and allowing them to impede us from moving forward is even worse.

If you have regrets that come to mind fairly regularly, regrets that keep dragging you back into bad memories and a painful past, ask yourself if there is any way your regrets can be corrected or resolved. I regret that in numerous instances I didn't deal with a particular situation as well as I could have. But those particular situations have long since passed and there are simply no corrections that can now be made. Other regrets, however, involve aspects that while they may not be erasable are certainly *correctable* in the sense that they can be addressed and put into a much more tolerable light than one of abject remorse, which is how we often view many of our regrets.

There have been numerous things that I have regretted not having done at an earlier time in my life, but I was able to resolve my regrets by simply doing, in time, what I had failed to do before. That is Rule #1 regarding regrets: *If you can "un-regret" them, do so.* Some regrets are simply lost to time and circumstance – *those* we just have to put behind us. Others, though, can be remedied by eventually addressing what we have continued to regret from the past.

Rule #2 is this: *If a regrettable situation is lost to time and circumstance, it is always wise to analyze it and determine what errors were made so that you will be unlikely to repeat the same errors again.*

Rule #3 – predictably I hope, is this: *If you have a regret that cannot be corrected and which is causing you to ruminate and obsess, it is time to put your regret in the proper perspective so that you are not impeded in your evolution – which means that, sometimes, the proper perspective for regret is one of pure acceptance.* Some things just can't be corrected, but acceptance *can* be a form of resolution.

If you regret, for example, that you didn't tell a family member how you felt about them before they went on a long trip overseas, write them an e-mail or text and tell them. But, if you didn't tell them how you felt about them before they suddenly passed away, well… tragically, that is a regret that is obviously more likely to pose a much greater degree of sadness and remorse. This is an instance in which one must be disciplined enough to accept the irrevocability of this regret and not allow feelings of guilt to keep one from moving forward. And while self-loathing and metaphorical self-flagellation over one's regretful omissions in this example may seem like the only behavior that can or should be justified, acceptance *is* the right answer. From a mental health perspective, choosing to put it in its proper place is the only way one can learn to be freed up from the terrible weight of this type and level of regret. You may not feel as though you have *the right* to move on, but the alternative is that you feel obligated to martyr yourself and suffer *indefinitely* because of a mistake that cannot be taken back.

I understand that self-imposed suffering for the purpose of penance feels logical and even *warranted*, and I am not going to question these feelings, as I have felt these very same things many times – punishing one's self for the pain one may have caused others often seems like a just thing to do. What I am suggesting is that punishing yourself for the rest of your life for something that simply cannot be corrected is not healthy or productive for you or for anyone else around you. You may not feel that you have the right to move on, but moving on is not the same as self-absolution. *Moving on is simply moving on.* It doesn't erase the past, and it doesn't necessarily forgive the past, but it does allow for you to have a future free of unflagging despondency caused by the regret that, thus far, you have been unwilling to let go.

If you have regrets that cause you anxiety, that cause you to dwell on past mistakes and that keep you in a phase of self-punishment, it's probably time to think about them from a perspective of correction or acceptance. Many things can be remedied – not made whole every time, of course – but they can often be made *better*. Those that can't be remedied must be accepted – accepted as a part of that past that you simply cannot fix – and no matter how sorry you may be, there are just no amends that can be made. These types of regrets have to be "written off" and chalked up to experience. But, in these instances, there is still some good that can come of things in that, if you will allow yourself, wisdom *can* be had from a time gone bad, and wisdom is a pretty good thing to walk away with, if you can moderate your guilt long enough to find the pearl.

Forget regret, or life is yours to miss.[27]

– Jonathan Larson

Chapter 16

Apologies

A good apology is several things. First, for it to be truly "good," it must be sincere. It must also be specific in the details of what you are apologizing for, it must be focused on *your* responsibility in whatever transgression may be involved, and, depending on the nature of the offense, a good apology often includes the assurance that "it won't happen again." It is *not* about the other person's actions or words (although there may well be relevant context provided by these). A good apology is straightforward, simple, and pure in its intent: to make amends for one's offense against the other person(s).

Here are several suggestions regarding apologies –

- If you're angry, don't apologize (assuming you are righteous in your anger)
- If it's really not your fault, don't apologize (but still try to work it out)
- If you're not sorry, don't apologize (but still try to work it out)
- If salvaging or repairing a relationship is not your desire, don't apologize
- The only thing worse than *not* apologizing for a wrong committed is a *poor* apology

No good comes from apologizing under these conditions. I'm not at all suggesting you should not consider reconciliation with the person – you absolutely should, if there is still a way to repair any trust issues – all I am saying is that apologies only "work" when one believes in the words and is completely sincere in the reasons for apologizing. But, please remember that the words of an apology do not automatically check the box for "doing all you can do." What checks the box is accepting responsibility (and whatever percentage of blame) and adding reconciliation to your overall efforts.

The only true apology is changed behavior.[28]

– J.S. Felts

A good apology need not be, but is *sometimes* loving or even affectionate – but it is *always* respectful, kind, gentle, and most importantly, *humble*. A good apology is about baring one's face, in spite of the pain, the embarrassment, and the regret, and saying, "I am wrong and I admit it." But it is not just about taking responsibility. It is also very much about reconciliation – a balancing of the ethical books, as it were. A good apology is about virtue and personal *honor*.

In our society, "honor" is something that is discussed quite a lot. It is most often associated with higher-order things like serving one's country, for example – and I am not opposed to it being associated with such noble endeavors, of course, but honor does not restrict itself only to those constructs we tend to put on a public pedestal. Honor is many things, and many of these things are not particularly magnanimous or audacious or heroic (per se) at all. Honor, in its simplest form, is about principle, integrity, truth, and genuineness – and these are the foundations of both *why* and *how* we should apologize when an apology is due.

How is this topic related to mental health and happiness? Mental health is very often about resolving conflict – conflict with another person and often within one's self – and nothing resolves conflict like a sincere apology. Apologies heal. They heal relationships, they heal the conscience, and they heal the soul. Apologies and *amends* "make things right." They bring about harmony and good will and peace of mind, and *that* is mental health. And, mental health is happiness.

Chapter 17

Stagnation and Burn-Out

Stagnation has many faces: boredom, lethargy, loss of interest, going nowhere, lack of direction, and so on. It's very common, stagnation is, and can very easily become a tepid bath of complacency – not unlike the proverbial frog in the proverbial boiling pot. It's a gradual process – one that sneaks up on us slowly.

People become stagnant in many aspects of their lives (i.e., work, health/fitness, relationships, intellectual growth, etc.), and, generally, the factors leading to stagnation are several. Let's discuss some of them, and for the purpose of this discussion, the area of stagnation discussed will be called *"X."* You may fill in the *"X"* with any area as may relate to your own life.

- Loss of former discipline regarding X
- Lack of interest in X due to a change in priorities
- A build-up of worries and anxieties that usurp your attentions from X, causing X to be marginalized
- Lack of confidence in your ability to make a change in the context of X
- Belief that doing *nothing* is better (or just more comfortable) than making a change in X
- Hoping that things will change on their own with X
- Not wanting to be involved in X (anymore or in the first place) but are afraid to make the break

This list is intentionally general. It is such because I didn't want a given reader to think that my objective was to write only about a particular type of stagnation. My intent was to address stagnation broadly so as to connect with as many people as possible. However, in doing it this way, no connection may be made at all because there just isn't enough context for anyone to apply these generalities in a more personal way. In an effort to avoid this possibility, let's look at a specific example of "real world" stagnation.

A few times a year, I talk to individual employees about stagnation at work. The conversations are always quite similar. The person is bored, tired, unhappy, doesn't see any change on the horizon, and can't imagine doing the job for two more years, much less the rest of their career. But, the person either doesn't have any real interest in another job, doesn't think any are available, doesn't think they have a good résumé, doesn't think they would be supported in a career move, and so on. Typically, what the person talks about are all the reasons they are stuck in a rut but none of the ways they propose to get out of it. They see "no change on the horizon" but don't seem able or motivated to try to change the horizon itself. I am not unsympathetic at all. I am merely pointing out that inaction rarely results in a spontaneous or miraculous change.

The *bad* news, as noted, is that stagnation is both common and easy to slip down into. The *good* news is that there is a way for swimming out of it. Ahead is the process of extrication and all it takes is a little effort and a decision to stop the clock and devise a new horizon (this isn't just "fluff" – I have known more than a handful of people that have done this successfully). Here's how you can do it, too:

1) Tell yourself today is *the day* and commit to making a change
2) Assess what you don't like about *X* and decide how it can be resolved
3) If there is no way to correct *X*, develop a strategy for finding a *new X*
4) If there is no new *X* to be had, make efforts to find *X* elsewhere
5) Address whatever other elements in your life may be preoccupying your mind and put them to bed. You can't get out of *Rut X*, if you are also trapped in *Ruts A, B, C,* and *D*.
6) Stop doing nothing and make something happen (doing nothing is how you got where you are today)
7) If you are not in a position to un-stagnate by yourself, talk to someone who can help facilitate

This straightforward process works for any area of stagnation, not just work. And, like a first-aid cream, just apply where needed.

Figuratively speaking, Day 1 of your slow descent into stagnation led to Day 311 (or maybe it was much sooner), which led to full-on stagnation. It may take 311 days (or many fewer) to become stagnant, but it only takes a few days to start reversing things. *Stop the clock.* No more indecision, no more excuses, no more wishful thinking, no more worry. Doing nothing will only mire you deeper, and each day will be another day wasted. Time is so patently limited, and there are very few things in life *not* bound up in time. Pick a day. Stop the clock. Restart your life. Stop *waiting* for a new horizon to appear and *make* it appear, instead.

Do not wait to strike till the iron is hot; but make it hot by striking.[29]
[Attributed to many, but the earliest rendition is believed to be by
Geoffrey Chaucer in *The Tale of Melibeus*
from The Canterbury Tales]

Now let's discuss "burn-out." For purposes of this chapter, burn-out at work, for example, is a feeling of exhaustion, a complete lack of motivation, a feeling of not being able to care or a *decision* not to care anymore because you have given all you are able to give. This feeling can be both physical and mental and tends to be a combination of both. Burn-out occurs when there is seemingly nothing left to burn. The objective of this chapter is to help you address burn-out and get the flame back alight.

Burn-out on the job is ultimately caused by stress. It's that simple. So, any discussion of burn-out, whether at work, home, or elsewhere, should be focused on stress, its causes, and ways to cope with it. Let's first discuss two basic kinds of stress.

Stress comes from one of two directions, and for the truly hard-core, *both* directions. There is self-imposed stress and stress from outside sources. It appears to me that most people are stressed primarily by outside sources, but I observe other people that are stressed by pressures of their own making, as well. The larger group comprises those that feel stressors coming from their environment and not necessarily from the inner chambers of their psyche. The external stressors that I most commonly see are related primarily to 1) supervisor-subordinate relationships and 2) environmental conditions (i.e., work assignments).

As I begin the discussion of supervisory-subordinate relationships, I want to be very clear that I have no bias for or against either side. As a consultant, advisor, and peer counselor I have seen both sides at fault many times. As with all human relationships, sometimes one side is at fault, sometimes it's the other side, and sometimes, it is a combination. Whatever may be the case in your particular circumstance, you can easily apply the guidance here, as it addresses all three possibilities.

If you are "stressed out" by your supervisor, for example, it has been my observation that the two most common problems are these: Either there is a communication problem (that can absolutely be resolved) or you are very likely not the best employee you can possibly be. I am not saying that there are not really bad supervisors out there. Of course, there are, but it is rare, in my experience – almost unheard of, in fact – for truly excellent employees to have problems with their supervisors, even when those supervisors are not very good or are even very bad. So, let's talk about these two categories of stress causation.

If you are always butting heads with your supervisor and you *really are* a very good employee, then my money is on a communication problem. Either they are not *aware* of what you are producing *or* you are producing something that is not what they have asked for or want. On more than one occasion, I have spoken to employees who have told me about the good work they are doing, only to tell me minutes later that the supervisor isn't asking for *XYZ* "but they really should be." Although that may well be, giving the supervisor *XYZ* when they are asking for *ABC* is definitely going to cause problems for you. Communication in this instance is imperative. If you are not going to give them what they want, then you should be trying to persuade them to want something different. All it takes is a conversation.

If, however, you are stressed out by your supervisor because they are always "on your back," it would make sense to ask yourself honestly if you are truly an excellent employee. If you probably aren't, make the necessary adjustments and supervisory complaints will evaporate, as will your stress. And, yes, it really is that simple (unless your boss is just mean for the sake of it, which is very, *very* rare).

Now let's talk about external conditions. Let's say you have a pretty good relationship with your supervisor, for example, but your environment is not good. That's a different kind of stress, but which can be just as taxing, and which can also be remedied, most of the time, by communication. Are you tired of the actual work, are you bored with the subject matter, or have you simply done that particular job too long? Does your chair hurt your back, do the lights above you flicker, is the person you have been assigned to work with driving you nuts? Whether the problem seems big or small, waiting for it to change on its own will likely prove to be a very long wait. If something in your environment is causing you stress, it only makes sense to discuss it with someone. Usually, your supervisor is the best person to start with. If not, then determine who the best person is and initiate the conversation. Change happens quickest when you *cause* it to happen. Now, let's talk about the other kind of stress – the *self-imposed* kind.

While self-imposed stress *should* be the easiest to curtail, it is very often the most difficult. Humans are strange, peculiar, mysterious creatures who do very strange, peculiar, and mysterious things, and self-imposed stress for some is just part of everyday life, no matter how illogical it may be. There are more than a few people I have encountered over the years that either *come* to work stressed out or *get* stressed out after they get there. But, however their stress may come about, their stress levels are mostly of their own making. Perfectionism, insecurities of all types, guilt complexes, and fear are common reasons that people push themselves harder than anyone around them is asking them to push. If you are burned out at work, home, or wherever, ask yourself these questions?

- Am I working hard because I want to be excellent, or am I working hard to be liked/loved?

- Am I working more than 8-10 hours a day because it is truly required, or because I don't want people to think I leave before *all* the work is done?
- Am I burned out by the family because I do all the work, or am I burned out because I do not relax, and/or never ask others for help?
- Do I work hard because the work improves things that need improvement, or am I doing the hard work because it feeds my self-esteem by being known as a very hard-worker?
- Am I working this hard because my boss or someone else will be disappointed in me if I don't, or am I doing it because if I don't, I will be disappointed in myself?
- How much of my efforts are based on obsessive-compulsive tendencies, and how much are based on reasonable and actual need?
- Am I working this hard because if I don't do it, it won't get done, or because I am unwilling to complain or ask for help?
- Are the expectations I have of myself a *reasonable* 5% higher than others' expectations or an *unreasonable* 50%?
- Who is inciting or causing me to work so strenuously every day, me or someone else?
- Am I the "victim" of a stressful environment, or have I caused my stress by making the standard for achievement unreasonably high?
- Am I being a martyr, or is the pace and volume of work I am committing to truly necessary?
- Am I striving every day for excellence or am I trying to be perfect?
- Am I in a position to righteously complain, or has complaining about how much work I have to do become part of my identity?

Many people that are stressed out by their jobs are really stressed out by the way they *choose* to manage their jobs. They are stressed out, and over time, *burned out* because they, for various reasons, won't allow themselves to work at a reasonable pace and volume. These people are really just perfectionists in hard-workers' clothing, and perfectionism can very easily be the source of burn out. It's great to pursue excellence – I preach this philosophy regularly – but excellence is not perfection, nor is "awesome," "exemplary," or "outstanding." *Perfection*, by any reasonable standard, is unattainable, so it is very important to be careful not to get sucked into an obsession with it. Trying to reach perfection *will* burn you out and drive you mad. Trying to be awesome and excellent and exemplary, on the other hand, is good and healthy and valuable. By all means, do the latter and not the former.

If you are burned out, I have good news for you: It's a fixable condition 90%-95% of the time. If your burn-out derives from stress that comes from your environment, then you can try to adapt to it, of course, or you can try to change it. Making an environmental change, almost always involves a conversation, and *reluctance* to have such a conversation (as so many seem to have) is the same as a reluctance to seek out change. If you want something to be different, most of the time you must ask for it. If your burn-out derives from self-imposed stress, then you must change your ways, your standards, your insecurities, your perceptions, or whatever makes sense, so that what used to stress you out is no longer allowed to. One must either change the elements of stress or change the way one chooses to cope with those elements. Ultimately, it comes down to one basic philosophical question: *Are you burned out because of the stressors life has imposed on you, or are you burned out because you are not coping with the stressors of life in a logical, prudent, and sensible way?*

Stress is real. We all deal with it every day to one degree or another. But stress does not automatically lead to burn-out. It can be managed, but it requires our engagement, self-care, and effort, usually in the form of directed communication with someone that can help us facilitate things *or* an effort to change the way in which we perceive ourselves, our responsibilities, our standards and the ways in which we identify and cope with stress. Burn-out, on the surface, may appear to be all external and situational, but it is almost always within our own power to prevent and/or change.

Burnout, like any difficult experience, is a great teacher.
My question is, "What is it trying to tell you?"[30]

— Dr. Rebecca Ray

Chapter 18

Less Philosophy, More…Something

I've been laying a lot of psychology/philosophy on you for the last many pages, so I thought maybe I would lighten the mood a little. If you grin at this, then I have accomplished my objective. If you "*LOL*," then I overshot. In any event, the purpose of this so-called "chapter" is to give you a short break from the weight of the previous ones.

I send my family and friends a lot of texts. I enjoy it. I do not have the *RAM* on this computer and you do not have the time to read *all* the absurd texts I send them, so I thought I would give you some of the ones that might be of vague interest.

My family has been the victim of my dubious "comedy" since I was relatively young, and over the years, I must assume (based on the limited feedback I receive from them) that the cumulative effect of it has taken its toll. Fortunately for me and unfortunately for them, I do not require much affirmation (if any, frankly), which condition allows me to continue to text them prolifically without the least bit of concern about their lack of consistent or interested replies. Most of the time, they don't even *feign* an interest, which makes me laugh all the more *('cause, sometimes, you just gotta entertain your ownself)*.

Here are some of the tales that I have told them by text. Typically, I go into great detail in these texts. Lucky for you, however, I am presenting only the *abbreviated* versions…

- I have a *three-story* pool. I texted my sister this after she told me they had just put in a pool of their own
- I am going to open a shop called *Shim It*, based on the notion that all the scrap wood I have lying around could make me *massive* profits if sold commercially, because everyone needs to shim up something, eventually
- I street race every Thursday night in a 1997 Sebring, and I won't disclose the location because it's illegal

- I got a really good deal on a boat [boat people and a lot of *non*-boat people should get the humor of this one, equally]
- I admonished them about using *Corn Nuts* in place of corn pops as cereal, because, well… they just don't pair up with milk as well, of course
- I am opening yet *another* store called *Tactical Smoothies* [the joke is probably on me, though, because this would probably work]
- After my sister sends me some video or a meme that is obviously funny, I will reply that *"I really don't care for that type of humor"* even though it is the same type of humor I often send to her
- I feed my borrowed cat (it's the neighbor's, but he seems to like my place better) Pop-Tarts and Reese's Pieces (which I insist on pronouncing "Reecees Peecees" and insist they pronounce it that way, too)
- When I get a text from close friends or family, I sometimes say that I'm too busy to talk because of my Zumba class or that I'm updating my Facebook page or doing a TikTok video (none of which I have ever done, ever, although I am not at all judging anyone who does)
- A few days ago, I told my nieces I was so drunk that I mowed the neighbor's fence (not the *grass* on the fence line – the fence itself) around midnight and was mad because the neighbor's dogs starting barking at me
- I asked my brother-in-law to buy a portable generator for me so that we could play full-size, arcade-grade air hockey at an annual Fall campout I have had for the last 30 years with nine other close friends of mine [You don't get it? Well, that's because it's idiotic. It's not *classically* funny. It's *stupid*-funny. OK, maybe it's just funny to me…]
- In *another* campout-related text – this time regarding a Spring-time campout for the grown kids in the family – I proposed several themes for a camp out: A cake or cupcake TV-show theme, a Parliament theme, a Frieda Kahlo theme, a Jersey

Shore theme (the camp out is in Oklahoma), or a Disney theme [I so hope for you, the reader, that the ridiculousness of a themed camp out translates from the page to your mind. With any luck, your mind is *at least* 10% as warped as mine]

- I have been drunk-dialing a woman in Albuquerque every Thursday night and was recently charged with a misdemeanor for harassment because they caught me... because I didn't know they had Caller ID there

- Due to the popularity of putting Ranch dressing on almost everything, I am going to establish a roadside network of Ranch dressing kiosk dispensers. I have not decided on the fee yet [once again, the joke may very well be on me, as I suspect there are at least a few of you shrugging your shoulders and saying, "I would actually use one of those..."]

Yes, I know these are all far more stupid than funny. That's the whole point, for better or for worse. I have at least a thousand more of these gems, but I know 99.89% of you did not come here to be entertained, so I will move on. For those that didn't appreciate this comedic interlude, I apologize and will get back to the psychology/philosophy stuff right now...

Chapter 19

Loneliness

Loneliness is one of the most difficult emotional states we humans have to deal with. I suspect between 91.3% and 95.7% (I like odd numbers) of us prefer to be connected to others at some level and degree. Although the preference or perceived need for human interaction is certainly on a spectrum, there is only a very, very low percentage of people who are at the end of the spectrum where *no* form of human society is preferred. We are quite simply a species that likes to be with each other most of the time. It is part of our DNA. Which means that when we are alone *and* feeling lonely, we feel uneasy and anxious, because our DNA just doesn't like it (much the same as we do not like the dark, for example) – it is simply not a state of being we are comfortable with. Hopefully, you will notice that I italicized the "and" a few lines above to highlight the important distinction between being alone and being lonely. They are not the same thing for many people (namely for introverts), though we all know people that *are* lonely almost any time they are alone. But, whether you are often lonely or seldom so, loneliness is a reality for many of us at some point in our lives, so it is important that we learn coping skills that typically do not come very natural to us. With this in mind, there are, generally speaking, two basic ways of coping with and managing loneliness: 1) learning to be more comfortable with being alone and/or 2) finding ways to become more connected to individuals and society in general.

As with any condition that we are not naturally good at enduring, learning to be comfortable when we are alone takes practice. I am not suggesting we should *proactively* cause ourselves to be alone in order to become better at it but rather that when we *are* alone, we should take time to *be* in our aloneness instead of trying to repress or avoid our feelings of loneliness. To become more comfortable with aloneness/loneliness, we must make a focused effort not so much to embrace the loneliness but, instead, to get more comfortable with our feelings about it. You might think of it like learning to tread water and coming to feel at ease with it, even though it is not our favorite activity.

Early on, as we first begin learning to be comfortable in the water, the idea of being thrown into the deep end makes most of us dreadful and afraid. And in these early stages of learning, when we do find ourselves in the deep end, the last thing we are thinking about is learning to *stay* in the deep end by learning to tread water. Instead, we are doing everything we can to leave and return to the shallows. But in learning to become comfortable with deep water, we learn that while being in the deep end may still make us a bit uneasy, learning to tread water makes things quite bearable and not so dreadful at all. We don't necessarily love it, but we learn to be fairly comfortable with it.

The majority of us tend to treat loneliness the same way as we do deep water. Once we feel it, we usually run from it by busying ourselves with tasks, making phone calls, shopping, watching movies, etc. – anything we can do to avoid the anxiety of being alone. So, just as with our deliberate decision to learn to be more comfortable in the water, it is also easy enough to make the same decision about learning to be alone. With a little practice and discipline, we get to the state of mind in which deep water does not cause us to panic; likewise, solitude need not cause anxiety in us due to loneliness. Treading in the anxiety of loneliness, staying in it until we are calm, learning to manage our feelings as we exist in our solitude is how we become more at peace with it. Running from these feelings, leaving the deep end to go where it is more comfortable will not teach us anything or make us stronger. So that loneliness does not overtake us emotionally, we must be willing to fight through the anxiety until repetition and familiarization take the angst away – just like learning to tread water in the deep end.

> *If you're lonely when you're alone, you're in bad company.*[31]
> – Jean-Paul Sartre

Something my counselor friend Shaun mentioned to me is that he uses his alone time as a way of preparing for those times when he *won't* be alone. For instance, being alone might be a good time to exercise, to watch the show or movie that those around you may not want to watch, to get things ready for work on Monday, or to do some chore that is less likely to get done when one should be considering the needs of others when they are around. This is not just "busy work," but rather it is an opportunity to work towards something on the horizon for the sake of others. In this way, though you are working on it alone, you maintain a feeling of connectedness to those you care about and who care about you.

The other way of coping with loneliness involves learning to better connect with those around us. And while this may sound a little easier to implement than learning to be alone, for some, this coping strategy is actually often *more* difficult. It typically just depends on one's personality. Those more prone to gregariousness find this path to be much more palatable, while those more prone to shyness typically do not tend to like this avenue at all.

There are many reasons people may feel shy:

- Sometimes when our self-esteem is not very good, we feel vulnerable, so we avoid others so as not to risk criticism/rejection
- Depression very often causes people to avoid others
- Poor health/low energy can obviously make us feel as though we do not have the strength to be with others
- Poor self-image and not feeling "good enough" to interact with some people tends to make us behave in a shy manner
- Personality/DNA can be innate reasons for shyness

Whatever it may be that makes you feel reluctant to engage with others, you can overcome it, if you are truly willing to make an effort. You are not stuck with "that's just who I am." None of us are. If you want to make a change, then make a change. It doesn't require a lot of prep or a lot of psychology. All it takes is *the flip of a switch*. All you have to do is *decide*.

You want to start saving more money? *Then do it*. You want to be more disciplined about exercising? *Then do it*. You want to start trying to be more engaged with the world, meet new people, be less alone? *Do it.* Make an effort. Start today. All you have to do is decide. And why not? What you have been doing must not be getting you any nearer your objective, so doesn't it make sense to try something new? *Take a chance.* Be different than you were before. Being the same won't solve the problem. I'm not saying it's easy. I know that it isn't. But whether something is black diamond difficult or green circle easy (why I used ski slope difficulty ratings here, I don't know) isn't relevant if you truly want to accomplish something.

When they were discussing the first international space station all those years ago, I doubt that the guy in the back that said, *"Ummm, yeah, I don't know… this sounds pretty hard…"* was the person they put in charge, assuming he was allowed to keep his job at all. And I don't even want to think about the guy who said this same thing when they were getting ready to build the pyramids... Yes, yes, yes, changing our behavior, motivating ourselves to do things we haven't done before is difficult. But if it were easy, you would already be doing it. So… do you want to stay lonely for the rest of your life, or do you want to make a few minor adjustments to your weekly habits and change the way you live? Well, all you have to do is flip the switch.

Loneliness is a bad feeling. No one likes it. But being alone doesn't mean that you have to feel lonely, *and* just because you tend to be shy or have poor self-esteem, for example, doesn't mean you were predestined to be alone or sentenced to loneliness. *You weren't* and *you aren't.* We may not have a choice in some things (there are *some* circumstances outside our control), but we *all* have a choice in how we choose to perceive the world, how we allow the world to treat us, and how we choose to behave in it. If you're lonely and don't like it, cinch up your belt and endeavor to make some changes that will make you feel less lonely. You can wait for a one-in-a-million miracle to magically change your circumstances, or you can take charge of your life and reduce the odds dramatically by *making* things happen. Sure, it might be difficult, but I assure you it will be worth the effort. All you have to do is make a sincere and dedicated effort. What are you waiting for? What have you got to lose? *Flip the switch.*

Chapter 20

Forgiveness

Injustice is an abhorrent thing. It is one of those things that, no matter what form it takes, is repugnant to all of us. But, as we have been told since we were very young, *life isn't fair.* Well, sometimes it is, of course, but the point is, *sometimes it's not.* More specifically, *humans* are not always fair. Most humans are good and decent, but sometimes, people just aren't very nice and sometimes they do unfair and unjust things.

The need for fair play and justice is in our DNA, "in our bones," as they say. It is hard-wired in 99.37% of us (give or take). And when we don't receive it, we naturally rail against it like nothing else. What's right is right, and what's wrong, well… *makes us really mad.* And why shouldn't it? Being wronged just isn't right, and when it happens to us, we want to set things straight, makes things even, balance the scales of justice, as it were. And every now and then, we can.

Sometimes, when we are wronged, we *do* get to even the score. If someone backs into our car at the store, for example, and it gets reported, insurance pays for it, and everything works out fine – *back to even.* If we get blamed for something we didn't do and the real culprit comes forward, we get an apology from the accuser, and the misunderstanding goes away – *back to even.* But sometimes our car gets hit, the perpetrator *doesn't* come clean, and it's our own insurance that pays the bill. And, sometimes we are the victim of underhandedness, defamation, or some other dishonesty, and a misunderstanding persists to the point that our reputation is unfairly damaged and no recourse can be found and no remedy is ever delivered. In instances such as these, the justice to which we are entitled just can't be claimed. It's unfair and it's maddening and it's wrong, but justice, regardless of the realm, is simply never guaranteed.

Humans are a fallible lot. With humans, errors are inevitable, and sometimes our errors hurt people. And, sometimes these "errors" aren't errors at all. Sometimes people act deliberately to hurt us, and our sense of justice is stirred even more intensely. Yes, people *are* "the worst," as it is often humorously said, and when we are wronged, whether by mistake or by intent, most of us get very upset when it happens. Sometimes when a transgression occurs, we get so upset that we become enraged and we find it difficult to think of anything else, and sometimes this fixation lasts for a very long time. I'm sure all of us know people that have been angry at an old friend or a family member for 10 or 20 years, or perhaps *we* are that angry person. Such a scenario (one in which the anger lasts for years) isn't hard to imagine when one party has truly been wronged and when no amends have been made. Without justice, there isn't much motive for people to forgive. It's unfortunate and sad, but there *is* a certain logic to this lack of forgiveness in that forgiveness typically follows an attempt to return the justice that was stolen.

When there *is* contrition, though, humans are pretty good at forgiveness – sincere remorse, apologies, etc. tend to cause the offended to feel some sense of compassion or clemency or mercy. In these instances, humans are often very quick to forgive because they feel that, by way of an apology, at least a percentage of justice is being restored.

As we all know and have felt, *acknowledgement* is a very important part of an apology – stating out loud that what was done wrong was, in fact, wrong. It is this combination of apology and genuine remorse that seems to be the best catalyst for inciting forgiveness. I don't know too many people so hardened that an admission of guilt and a heartfelt apology won't soften. Sometimes, though, people *intend* to wrong others, and in those instances, there is no apology and there is no contrition. Sometimes people do things that we find unforgiveable. Some things people do are so egregiously wrong that forgiveness can't even be contemplated. In these instances, the injustice is glaring and unequivocal. *And it is at this most illogical juncture that my argument for forgiveness enters.*

Forgiveness is a great thing – one of the greatest. Many of the world's religions, of course, include it as a central part of their doctrines. To my mind, the concept of forgiveness is one of the most noble and transcendent in the catalog of human triumphs – because it is a triumph over human nature itself. Humans, generally speaking, are not particularly *prone* to forgiveness. It is a concept that we are often taught, a concept that we *can* clearly learn, and one that we have adopted as a part of the principles that comprise what it is to be kind and compassionate and good. But, it is a concept that does not *feel* as innate, for instance, as the desire for companionship or the desire to be creative. Forgiveness takes effort. And sometimes *a lot* of effort. Mostly because in order to embrace it, one has to overcome the tremendous gravity of anger caused by injustice and because it doesn't *feel* as though it is consistent with the application or the balance of justice.

Let's say that one of your kids gets hurt at a birthday party at a neighbor's house, sustaining a serious injury caused by the child of the neighbors themselves, and the neighbor offers no apology, does not offer to cover the medical bills, and has lapsed homeowner's insurance, leaving you to pay for everything. When something inexcusable like this occurs, it takes very little time for anger, resentment, and animosity to eclipse any feelings of neighborliness, much less forgiveness. Or perhaps the pool guy comes to your house, and even though you asked him numerous times to keep the back gate closed, he still forgets and lets the dog out, who runs away and is, unbearably, never seen again. It should not have happened, it was terribly irresponsible, unfair, and inexcusable, and no matter how bad he feels, the pool guy does not *deserve* your kindness. You have lost a member of your family and you are in pain…

Now, let's say that months after the birthday party, you were never compensated for your child's medical bills and the injury never healed properly, or, after the pool guy came and your dog was let out and never returned, you simply cannot find "closure." Where is the peace? Where is the peace five months or five years later? Forgiveness is not owed or deserved. Where is the justice? *Ten* years later and you are still angry – because there is no justice and no justice is forthcoming. You were wronged and nothing's going to fix that. It is completely unfair.

Completely. Although justice isn't guaranteed, it is *deserved,* and when it is withheld, when we are cheated out of it, bitterness, anger, and resentment surely follow – which is the epitome of insult on top of injury. The unfairness in and of itself is bad enough, but having to cope with the anger and the hurt and the aggravation day after day is double the offense.

Forgiveness is a very simple process. It couldn't be simpler, actually. Unfortunately, the human psyche complicates it terribly. In practice, all it takes is a decision. It's binary – *on or off* – like so many other things, and you can just flip a switch – if you choose to. What makes it so difficult for us to forgive is our innate need for justice – the "logic" I spoke of earlier that tells us that forgiveness doesn't really make sense – and, of course, the big one: *pride.* And while these three are all immense and difficult to overcome, the benefits of forgiveness to our mental health are even bigger.

To understand an advocacy for forgiveness, in general, and to better understand my promotion of it, specifically, it is helpful to think of forgiveness in the same way, in the same context that we think of a gift. When we give someone a gift, we give it out of kindness. We give a gift without an expectation of reciprocation. We give a gift simply because we want to and not because the recipient deserves or has earned it. A gift, theoretically, is given because it is generous to do so and simply because we can – *no strings attached.* Forgiveness, I think, should be bestowed in the very same way. And, although a lot of people might be considered kind and generous, I would argue that a far smaller percentage of people are truly forgiving, and this is probably due to the fact that the sticking points I mentioned in the previous paragraph really *are* extremely difficult to overcome.

Why would we want to forgive someone who has wronged us, especially one who may have wronged us intentionally? There just isn't any logic in it. Why would we want to forgive someone who isn't remorseful, who doesn't like us, and who doesn't care if we ever speak to them again? What possible reason is there for forgiving someone who is completely undeserving of our mercy, undeserving of the gift of forgiveness? The answers are – 1) You wouldn't want to; 2) There isn't any logic in it; and 3) There really isn't any *good* reason for it. *Except that it is the only thing in the world that can give you back your peace of mind.*

For forgiveness to have a benefit – for it to "work" – one has to believe and embrace that forgiveness, when given sincerely, is a true gift. Forgiveness is also a *write-off*. It is an act that says, *"Your debt is forgiven and we will not be asking for repayment in the future."* Forgiveness is a dusting of the hands that says, *"It's over. I'm over it. I'm moving on. It is not worth any more of my time or energy."* Forgiveness is an act of generosity that says, *"You used to owe me, but now you don't, and I no longer care about the 'debt.'"* But more than anything, forgiveness, *genuine* forgiveness, is a *pardoning*. It doesn't erase the past (because nothing can), but it treats the future as if the past had never occurred. When one forgives with a truly generous heart, the anger and all the other emotions that come with it are released into the ether along with the forgiven debt. Forgiveness does *not* restore justice; it merely makes the pursuit of justice no longer relevant.

> *To forgive is to set a prisoner free and discover*
> *that the prisoner was you.*[32]
>
> – Lewis B. Smedes

When something happens to you that is wrong, unfair, unjust, and when that thing cannot be reversed, when justice cannot be delivered, one has but two choices: To 1) begrudge the loss of justice, to lament it, and obsess over it, or, 2) *let it go.* You can hang onto your pride, your logic, your sense of fair play and justice and be miserable but righteous and justified, *or* you can relinquish your pride, your logic, and your reasons and *be at peace*. There *is* no logic in it. The person does *not* deserve it, and it *is* incongruous to give someone a gift in return for the theft of justice. But forgiveness was never supposed to make sense. Give it because you can. Give it because it is magnanimous. Give it because it is cleansing, liberating, and heartening. And give it because it will return to you the peace of mind that you lost and won't get back without it.

Chapter 21

Boundaries

One of the things I talk to people about fairly regularly are relationship boundaries. Whether the boundary issues are between family members, significant others, co-workers, or friends, the problem is almost always the same: One person in the relationship is being pushed in a particular area and to a degree that is beyond what they are comfortable with. We all have *some* boundaries, but boundary *problems* arise because we have either not made our boundaries clear, or we have made them known but have failed to enforce them. Boundary issues are a source of constant anxiety for a lot of people across many age groups and populations. If you want to feel better about yourself and attain a greater sense of peace, addressing boundary issues is imperative if you are going to have harmony in your relationships. In my estimation, boundaries are one of the most beneficial yet least discussed aspects of most relationships, so I felt that a chapter devoted to the topic was important.

I think of relationship boundaries as interpersonal rules of conduct. Sometimes these rules come about very naturally. When they do, they do so in an easy, "organic" manner due to the fact that both parties see the world, social ethics, and equality in relationships, for example, from the same general perspective. In these instances, no boundaries really need to be discussed at all because both parties already play by the same rules. Unfortunately, however, not everyone does play by the same set of rules, so boundary discussions are often very important, especially in the beginning stages of a relationship, regardless of the type of relationship it may be.

Boundaries are very often, if not *most* often, about self-respect and self-esteem. If you don't respect yourself, you will not likely have good boundaries and you will allow others to push past your lines of comfort. So, if you value the other person more than yourself, and that person is exploitive (bullyish, manipulative, egotistical, etc.), you are going to have boundary problems. And the harsh reality is that many people will push you as far as you will let them. The "moral" here is that self-respect and self-worth will most often determine whether you set good boundaries or any at all.

Boundary difficulties are also often about guilt (legitimate or false), the avoidance of conflict, and the "need" to be loved or accepted. Feeling guilty about pushing back, about challenging someone you like and respect, or feeling guilty because you feel you owe the person a certain amount of deference (e.g., because it's a family member, someone who has helped you in the past, or because you have never pushed back before) is not a rational reason to feel guilty. Because boundaries are about your own personal set of parameters in various areas of emotional and social conduct, someone's position or their past support, for example, should not be relevant to whether or not you allow them to exceed your boundaries.

People also routinely allow others to cross their boundaries because they simply do not want to deal with conflict. Confrontation is relatively uncomfortable for 85% - 90% of people, I would estimate, so a lot of boundary problems result from a person choosing to remain silent while the other person is pushing beyond the line. Avoidance of confrontation often becomes a way of life, one that, by definition, causes you to consistently misrepresent how you feel and which leads to an ongoing undercurrent of aggravation due to your unwillingness to articulate the things you don't like about the other person's behavior. And, those that feel they need the other person's approval are reluctant to express any form of criticism for fear of losing the affirmation that comes from that person's affection or support.

Think of it this way, perhaps: Would you rather go through a short period of unpleasantness in discussing your boundaries, or would you rather continue to feel subjugated by your own need for the other person's approval? What most people do not consider is that it is very possible to have both – to set new boundaries *and* keep the other person's approval. It doesn't always work out this way, of course, but I cannot think of any instance in which at least *trying* for both conditions isn't well worth the effort.

Lack of boundaries or *unenforced* boundaries cause us to resent the other person and ourselves, but the likelihood of the other person's poor boundaries suddenly and spontaneously becoming healthy boundaries, are about $1/10^{th}$ of 1%, so it is incumbent on *us* to make the change. Setting boundaries is simple but not necessarily easy (a common refrain of mine). It is *simple* in that all it entails is telling the other person how you feel about their behavior and making clear to them your own preferences. For example, if your parents like to feed your kids junk food when the kids are at their house but you have asked them to feed them just like you do at home, the choices you offer your parents should be very straightforward: *"Please feed the kids as we have requested or they will not be allowed to come back."* This is a battle that parents (you) will win 98 times out of 100, because we all know that most grandparents will do almost anything to see their grandkids. *The key is not to cave.* The instant you compromise your standards, you have lost the battle. Set your boundaries and do not flinch. If someone disrespects them, there must be some form of repercussion or enforcement, or the boundaries might as well not exist.

One of the most vital aspects of setting good boundaries is to do so very early on in any relationship. I hope it is obvious that you have the right to set boundaries at any point you choose, even if it's very late in the development of your relationship; however, the longer you wait, the more difficult it will be to get things back to conditions you are happy with. If you wait twenty years into a marriage, for example, before you tell your husband that you don't like that he always chooses what you watch together on TV, it is going to be much more difficult to persuade him that your TV preferences are just as valid as his, given that you have changed the rules, as it were, very late in the process. This in no way diminishes the validity of your complaint, of course. It will simply make it more difficult to make new rules, in most cases.

Another thing that greatly helps in the establishment of boundaries is the use of language that is firm and unequivocal. Whether you are speaking or writing, it is very important to choose words that are definitive when you are asking someone for something that you want or need. The following statements are examples of *equivocal* language, all of which invite challenges to your intended boundaries by anyone who is prone to such:

- "I would prefer that you didn't get to work much after 8:30 a.m."
- "Would you mind not parking so close to my vehicle? It is very difficult for me to get out."
- "I would rather not have to pick you up so early. Is that okay?"
- "It might be better if we were to wait another week before we leave so that I can get a few more things done."

The following are better alternatives:

- "Please come in from now on no later than 8:15 a.m. Thank you."
- "When you park behind me, please do not park so close to my car so that I can get out easier. Thank you."
- "I cannot pick you up until 7:00 p.m."
- "I won't be able to leave for another week. I have several things I want to accomplish first."

Boundaries are about speaking up, requiring courtesy and respect, and about enforcing fair play. Poor boundaries cause dread, anxiety, and animosity. Good boundaries require self-respect and a little courage, and while setting boundaries is best at the beginning of a relationship, it is *never* too late to set them. Ask for what you want and deserve from others. If they are worth having as friends and loved ones, they will comply (assuming, of course, that your requests are reasonable). If they do not, does it not seem logical to ask yourself if they are really worthy of being part of the circle that you call "friends and loved ones." To my mind, the answer is very straightforward: Those who claim to care about you should also respect you and want for you what you want for yourself.

Now, let's discuss boundaries from a different perspective. Those that we apply to ourselves…

I know a lot of "people-pleasers," and I'm sure you do, too. You may very well *be* one yourself, and I can tell you that I used to be one, and I will expound on this a bit more, shortly.

Having boundaries that regulate (for lack of a better word) ourselves is just as important as establishing boundaries that regulate others. And it is not uncommon for those that do not set boundaries well with regard to others to also have difficulty in setting boundaries for themselves. This is because people-pleasers find it so hard to say no, in general.

There are several different reasons that people-pleasers struggle with regulating themselves and saying no, and these are the most common:

- They want to be agreeable
- They want to avoid anxiety, confrontation, a sense of intimidation
- They want to avoid disappointing others
- They claim or actually *convince* themselves that whatever the request, it is "no big deal" and that "they are fine with it"
- They think or fear that saying no isn't "nice"
- They have become accustomed to putting themselves second in most circumstances

The primary reason behind *these* reasons is, once again, almost always one of self-esteem/self-respect.

There is, obviously, nothing wrong with being generous, helpful, compassionate, and kind. These are *always* good things. But, often, these are really nothing more than self-made excuses for lacking the level of self-esteem that is required for a person to set healthy boundaries.

Self-esteem and self-respect are *crucial* for knowing how we want to be and *should* be treated by others. And just because we are willing to make sacrifices for others at the expense of ourselves does not mean that these sacrifices are healthy or wise.

Givers need to set limits because takers rarely do.[33]

– Rachel Wolchin

The perils of people-pleasing are several and great. Once you have established yourself with friends and family as someone who rarely, if ever, says no, you naturally create the expectation in them that whatever request they may make of you will be granted. Which, in turn, almost *predestines* you (because of your inability to put yourself first) to say yes to them. Self-esteem and self-respect are what allow you to have appropriate boundaries, the boundaries that empower you to say no by putting yourself first – by believing that your time and energies are just as valuable as theirs, and that declining their request is not unkind, selfish, or rude.

I am confident we would all agree that we can't do everything for everyone all the time, yet many of the people-pleasers I know do not live this belief at all. In fact, most of these people *do* try to do everything for everyone all the time, which, means that their lives are really not their own, *because they have chosen to be at the disposal of everyone but themselves.* This is Peril #1.

What I have also routinely observed is that when a people-pleaser finally *does* say no, they do not do so because of courage or a flash of self-esteem, but rather because they are willing to tell a lie with regard to why they claim they must decline. This is Peril #2: *Dishonesty due to the lack of self-esteem and courage that is required to give an honest declination.*

Non-people-pleasers will simply say, *"No I can't babysit your kids,"* or *"No, I do not want to travel to your destination wedding,"* or *"No, I do not want to loan my car to you."* And they can say these things because they respect themselves enough to know that whether or not the other person gets upset, they have every right to decline and that saying no does not make them a "bad person." People-pleasers, on the other hand, will often say no by asserting a *false* reason that most anyone would agree *outweighs* their request: *"I can't babysit your kids tonight because we think one of ours has the flu"*; *"We won't be able to make it to the wedding in Mexico because my Mother recently had surgery, hasn't been doing very well, and I don't want to be too far away"*; *"Our other car has been acting up lately, and I can't be stranded without a car, if the other one won't start."* None of these are true, but the people-pleaser chooses a lie over the truth because it relieves them of their own responsibility in saying no. In essence, the subconscious "logic" goes like this: *I don't want to say no to you, but I simply have no choice...*

And Peril #3 is that *not setting boundaries on your own commitments to others causes a people-pleaser to be in a perpetual state of dread,* even if only subconsciously. People-pleasers are more anxious than those who are not because the decisions they make are typically reactive rather than proactive. When the phone rings for someone who isn't a people-pleaser, it's just someone on the phone. For a people-pleaser, though, the fear is that the person calling is going to ask them to do something they don't want to do, and the anxiety and dread comes from not wanting to do whatever it is but knowing that they're going to do it anyway – or from having to come up with a fib as to why they can't do it.

All three of these perils can directly be tied to happiness (rather to *unhappiness).* Being at everyone's disposal takes away your freedom, and freedom, as I have already asserted, is central to happiness; being dishonest in making excuses might free you from the obligation but, in turn, burdens you with the guilt of a lie; and, living in a state of dread is about as *unhappy* as a person can get.

A few paragraphs above I mentioned that I used to be a people-pleaser, and I was – and it was all because of poor self-esteem. Now, though I often say yes to people when they need something from me, I do it because I can and I want to and not because of any fear that they might think less of me if I were to say no. The truth is that I do not like to say no to people. It pains me to one degree or another every time I feel the need to say no, but whatever the nature of the emotion I am feeling – whether it is a form of guilt or just simple disappointment in not being able to say yes – it is, *now,* mitigated, or perhaps *countermanded* by my preference for expressing my true desires, by doing only those things that I feel I am in a good position to do, and by whether or not I should really *be* doing it at all. I will explain:

In my mind, the best reasons to do things for people are because 1) I sincerely desire doing it, 2) I am practically and responsibly available to, and 3) because what they have asked of me is reasonable and/or necessary to be done. Again, I say yes a *lot* – at a ratio of around 50:1,

I would guess – but when I do, it's because all three of these conditions have been met.

I was talking with someone just the other night on this topic, and I mentioned that one of the principles that I apply when making decisions about what I can or cannot do for others is based, in part, on my other obligations. The person I was speaking to, like so many others, is in the habit of saying yes to almost everything, so what I told them is that there are no boundary concerns, generally speaking, as long as the things you say yes to do not infringe on the "rights" or the boundaries of others. For example, if you live alone, it is perfectly fine for you to come in to work after hours when the boss asks you to, if you can and sincerely do not mind (assuming the request is truly optional). However, if you have a family and the boss asks you to come back in to work just as you were sitting down to dinner or were engaging in family time, you should decline (again, if the boss's request is for a genuinely voluntary commitment), given that saying yes would *unnecessarily and unfairly* cheat your family out of their time with you. Now, if the circumstances were such that you worked for a boss that fired people because they did not work extra when called upon, I would say that you probably need to interrupt dinner and go back to work as requested. But I would add very quickly to this recommendation that you should also be looking for another job.

Setting boundaries is about courage and courage comes from self-esteem and self-respect, which is just another way of saying *knowing what you believe in, applying what you believe in, and knowing your worth.* Having these beliefs and self-assurances will give you the ability to set boundaries for others *and* for yourself. *Without* these, your boundaries will undeniably be set by others – because that is what you have allowed them to do.

Chapter 22

Counseling: Client Psychology

If at some point in your life you believe you would benefit from counseling, regardless of the area of concern, it is important to be mindful of the things that will make your experience in counseling worthwhile and effective.

One of the most important things you must commit yourself to, if you truly want to receive the full benefits of counseling, is being completely transparent and honest with your counselor, just the same, and for the same reasons, as you are with your physician.

If you go to your medical doctor because you are having, for example, severe headaches, nausea, fainting spells, and partial blindness in one eye, but you tell them only that your head hurts because you are afraid you will be diagnosed with a brain tumor if you give them more detail, your doctor won't be able to accurately diagnose you because you have left out several important facts. If you go to a counselor and tell them about relationship problems you are having, for example, but you fail to disclose some of the things that you are responsible for in the relationship for fear the counselor will "blame" you for your own troubles, you will not get accurate or valid guidance, and you will be wasting your money and your time.

Many people go to counseling because they want to be vindicated, because they want to get affirmation and agreement, and in seeking these things, they often skew the facts in order to elicit the responses they are looking for, responses that will make them feel better in the short-term. The same is true in the medical example above. If you tell the doctor only that your head hurts, you may walk away with a prescription and an innocuous diagnosis, which will naturally make you feel good in the moment, but, in the long-term, because you didn't reveal all the facts, you will continue to wonder if you *do* have a brain tumor, all the while your symptoms continue to get worse. Psychological concerns are no different. If you are going to go to the trouble of finding a counselor, spending time in session, and spending the money, it only makes sense to be as forthcoming as you can be.

Another important aspect of sound client psychology is the philosophy of personal responsibility. Sometimes people are victims – sometimes they are unlucky in life, and sometimes random things befall people, no fault of their own. But most of the time, the troubles we face in this life include at least *some* percentage of personal responsibility. That is, most of the time when we are in a bad way, the way we got there had something to do with our own actions. Taking responsibility for our actions is imperative in learning to adapt one's thoughts and behaviors to better, healthier, and more productive ones.

For example: Do you have a rude or mean boyfriend? Are you still with him? If you are going to counseling to discuss your relationship, you will not likely find a counselor willing to discuss your boyfriend's faults because *he* is not the client – *you* are. So, what the counselor will discuss is your own responsibility for your problems at home – meaning *not* that you are responsible for your boyfriend's bad behavior but rather that you are responsible for your own reactions to it and, thus, your own unhappiness. If you are going to tolerate his poor treatment of you, that is your choice, of course, but you must be willing to take responsibility for this choice. Yes, your boyfriend may be a "jerk," but you are the one who continues to abide his bad behavior. To be a good client, to be logical and objective in counseling, you must be willing to admit this and to accept responsibility for your part in your own discontent.

Another important mindset you should adopt when preparing to go to counseling, if counseling is going to benefit you at all, is that of being humble and accepting of assessment and critique. Good counselors take issue with faulty reasoning, poor logic, and missing facts. If the details of your discussion don't add up, or if the things that you perceive are not reasonable or rational, it is the counselor's job to point this out. So, if you go to counseling and persist in being thin-skinned, argumentative, or defensive, counseling will be of no value to you. If you are going to counseling to be agreed with and told how unfair the world is, you might as well save your money and go see an old, sympathetic, non-confrontational friend who will do the same for free.

Counseling is not always pleasant. It is often hard work and it is often humbling and even painful, sometimes. But remember why you are going: You are going because you decided that it was time to make a change. So, if a counselor just sits back and tells you that everything you are doing is *A-OK*, you will leave believing no changes are necessary, but you will leave with the very same problems you came in with. Counselors aren't harsh or aggressive in their critiques, but they are often frank – *because that's their job*. You are paying them to help you, and being "nice" (passive) and uncritical (silent) when they hear something illogical or irrational does not help you.

Here's another way to think of it: If you pay a professional editor or proofreader to review your book or résumé, for example, it doesn't make much sense for you to feel wounded or to complain when they find grammatical errors, problems with syntax, and other flaws. You are paying them to make suggestions and corrections, so isn't that what you want them to do? Or, would you rather have a résumé with only a few marks on it so that you can feel a little better about yourself? Hopefully, you perceive these questions to be as rhetorical as they are intended. Here's yet another way to think about things: If everything in your life was rolling right along, you wouldn't be looking for assistance, so you shouldn't be surprised or confounded or hurt when the counselor provides that assistance in the form of critical analysis. For objective, open-minded, humble people that are ready to make changes in their lives, counseling is not very painful at all. For those that are the opposite of these, counseling is going to be a bit uncomfortable.

If you are in this second group of clients, I recommend that you don't go to even one session. You are simply not ready. For counseling to work, you must be ready to listen and you must be willing to make changes to both thoughts and behaviors. The best client is not necessarily the smartest, the most intellectual, or the one most "in tune" with themselves. Many people are very self-aware but do not put their self-awareness into action. The *best* client is the one who listens with a humble mind/heart and is willing to apply what they have learned over time until they have successfully altered their perspectives and behavior. Counseling works and it works well for those that truly embrace it – same as exercise, same as studying for an exam, same as dieting, same as lots of things we do to improve ourselves. If you want to be a good client; if you want to get your money's worth from counseling; if you want to make changes and improve yourself as a person, all you have to do in counseling is be honest, humble, sincere, and committed to the process.

Wise people prefer to benefit from constructive criticism
rather than be ruined by false praise.[34]

– Shiv Khera

Chapter 23

A Personal Chapter

I was depressed from the age of around 14-15 to the age of 37. All day, every day. It was a very difficult time. But the fact that I was once depressed – believe it or not – is completely incidental to my writing about happiness. You may find it interesting (the depression) – and I suppose it is – but it has nothing to do with my motive for writing this book. But I'm getting ahead of myself.

At 15, I stumbled onto a book about depression (I do not recall the title). The more I read about it, the more certain I became that the book was talking about me and that *I* had this thing called "depression." I already knew the *word* at that age, but I did not really know what it was. I assumed, as so many people did then and as so many still do today, that "depression" is just another way of saying a person is "extremely sad" – which, as many of you know, is not accurate at all. The book I read described many aspects of depression, and I remember being amazed that on those pages were such articulate descriptions of the mysterious state of mind in which I had found myself imprisoned for the last year or so, at the time. And at that time, I remember feeling an odd sense of comfort that, although what I was feeling was big and over-powering, it was at least a *known* entity – people knew about it, were writing about it, and clearly knew how I felt – so it was less intimidating than something about which I/we knew nothing. In the same instant, however, it also somehow made things worse, as I realized that this thing was big enough and scary enough for people to be writing books about, something that I had had the blissful ignorance of knowing nothing about before, other than that something strange was plaguing my mind. In this way, the book was as enlightening as it was sobering.

During these early years, I mentioned my depression to only a very few people. I told a teacher I was close to, and I later told my Dad the summer I turned 16. I also told a close friend, who did the best he could to comfort me, as he tried to understand something that I understood only *slightly* better than he did (and only because it was happening to me). Teenage years are tough, as we all know, and depression didn't make it much easier, as you can imagine. But, I survived them without any obvious damage and went onto college where, though it did not become more pronounced *outwardly*, it became more and more difficult for me to "feel normal," I suppose is the best way to put it. And, as depression does with many people, it made me feel very insecure.

Even though I was very verbal and articulate in "regular life," I had debilitating stage fright and did my best to avoid classes that made class "participation" a percentage of the grade. Further, even though I knew *empirically* that I was not unattractive, I never *felt* attractive and was very nervous about meeting new people, especially girls. In closed circles, I was considered intelligent, popular, nice-looking, funny, and even charismatic, but in environments in which I was unknown, none of what I knew theoretically to be true gave me any comfort. The worst of it, in some ways, was that I was aware of this; that is, as I perceived things, I was the most ineffectual "popular" kid in any given circle. As far as I could tell, no college kid had *less* realized success – proportionate to his potential – than I did. And it troubled me every day – an albatross that never left my shoulder.

But, I was a very logical person, with an aptitude for psychology and self-analysis. And what I deemed at that time to be logical and good, sound "psychology" told me I could beat it, that I could *out-think* it, (even though I had long suspected that it was a "clinical" depression, a biochemical problem that was just part of my "make-up," as opposed to situational depression). I was also stubborn and prideful and vain, *and* I was the oldest sibling, all of which factors combined to make failure a non-option in my mind.

And so I didn't fail. For 22+ years, I quietly battled the heavy pall of depression each day and held just enough ground to keep from sliding backwards, though I certainly never gained any ground, either. My depression never got perceivably worse, but it also never got better. It was quite amazing, actually, as to how consistently gray and sterile each day was, no matter what the happenings of a particular day. It was the same bad day, all day, every day. I made no progress and I got no relief.

I do have some good memories from that period of my life. Depression was always in the background, but it did not incapacitate me. I had good relationships at home and at work, and I laughed and had fun, at times. But even during the times I was able to derive some level of gladness from one activity or another, the depression was always hovering above me like a dense gray haze with a dankness that permeated everything I was thinking about and doing. I could smile, but I was never happy. I was able to look forward to some things, but never thoroughly and not very often. I could be hopeful, but only in a theoretical sense. I never wanted to give up and I was never suicidal, but I did not like my life or my state of mind.

As a side note, I should tell you that besides pride, vanity, being the oldest sibling with a very strong sense of protectiveness to a younger brother and sister, and a refusal to fail, I was also *ignorant*. Had I known the depression was going to last 22 years, it is very possible I would not have been able to weather the storm as well as I did. But I *didn't* know, and each day, I had just enough theoretical hope that it might go away to enable me to make it to the *following* day. And it went on like this day after day, year after year. Until one day when I was 37.

On a Saturday many years ago, I called a close doctor friend of mine, a surgeon, and asked if he knew much about "the new SSRI (select serotonin reuptake inhibitor) drugs." Although at the time of my phone call, there had been SSRIs on the market for several years, their prominence seemed to have increased at that time, and I was suddenly hearing about them more and more, to the extent that I finally got more curious than not and inquired. Though not in his area of expertise, he said he had heard positive reviews of the drug, that they were very safe and were considered to be quite effective with limited side effects. After determining that the risks were low and the rewards potentially very high, I put my vanity aside (the same vanity that kept me afloat for 22 years but *also* the very same vanity that prevented me from trying an SSRI many years *earlier* because I didn't think I "needed" medication to beat the depression – because *I* was a "born psychologist...with two masters degrees in psychology/counseling, etc., etc.") and scheduled an appointment with a primary care physician to see about trying it out.

Well, long story short... *it worked*. Within two weeks of starting the medication, I felt... *different*. Dramatically. Often this type of medication takes up to six weeks to "kick in," but in my case, it was much quicker than is typical, which confirmed for me what I had always suspected: that it *was* a biochemical problem (else the medication would not have worked and worked so quickly). Needless to say, I was extremely encouraged, though not quite ready to be *too* hopeful regarding any would-be transformation.

After about a month or a little longer, I realized that although there was a marked change in my mental state, I didn't like the particular drug I was prescribed (the side effects were just too bothersome), so I asked the doctor if I could try another one. He agreed, and I started another SSRI immediately and within a very short time, it became clear that this one was a much better fit. After taking the new one for several months and assessing the benefits of varying dosages, I was able to determine that half of the lowest dosage of this second SSRI was all that I needed to keep the depression at bay. *Half* of a small pill. Twenty-two years of daily depression concluded in months by the ingestion of only a few milligrams of medication per day. And with respect to those people who inexplicably insist that medication for significant mental distress is unnecessary or even misguided, I can only assume that they have never been clinically depressed, for example, or are simply being disingenuous for the purpose of trying to advance whatever agenda they may have. Anti-depressants and other mental health drug therapies *do* work for many people (millions, in fact), and all it takes is an objective before-and-after observation of these people to know this to be true.

But before I close and tell you the point of this chapter, I want to also tell you what *isn't* the point. The point of this chapter is *not* that I used to suffer from depression and am no longer depressed. It is also not that I took medication and that I am better for having taken it. It is also not that depression is a horrible thing and that once it is gone, one can be happy. Nor is it that medication solves all depression (I assure you it doesn't). The point of this chapter is that I learned a great deal from being depressed, and though I would never wish it on anyone, I *did* learn a lot from it and am truly glad it happened to me. *Truly* glad. Because this is what I learned:

- That self-reflection and self-analysis are worth every minute you spend on them (so while you are unhappy, *study* your unhappiness instead of just trying to escape it)
- That the *suffering* mind is often far more in touch with humanity than the *contented* mind and because of this, suffering has great value, if one is willing to embrace this aspect of it while still endeavoring to heal
- That no matter what you may be going through, in good times or in bad, if you lose sight of your purpose, not much else matters and you are basically just walking in circles
- That managing one's emotions is possible, even in the midst of pain, as long as one is willing to make a concerted effort
- That even when you feel miserable, the most helpful thing you can do for *yourself* is to be kind and ethical to others
- That having low self-esteem causes one to be prone to insecurities, defensiveness as well as shyness, avoidant behavior, and self-isolation for purposes of self-protection
- That courage is something that you can have at any point in your life, even in the worst of times
- If you don't like yourself, it makes it difficult for others to like you, *not* so much because you are particularly unlikable but rather because your low self-esteem doesn't allow you to *feel* likable, nor does it allow you to fully *believe* others when they say they *do* like you
- You cannot be a *truly* good person if you are not happy. Being unhappy makes it very difficult to focus outside one's self, and even though I tried hard to dedicate myself to the philosophy of kindness during the time I was depressed, *succeeding* in being consistently kind, thoughtful, courteous, polite, and selfless was often very difficult because being unhappy is passively

demotivating of ethical behavior and it is just plain difficult to be cheerful when one is unhappy. So, while being kind and good is certainly possible, it is much more difficult to be such easily and faithfully when one isn't happy. In short, unhappiness causes one to be self-centered, and that is never good

- But the greatest thing I learned is that self-esteem/self-acceptance is the *single most important* pavestone on the path to happiness

During the entire time that I was depressed, I never observed or perceived the "mechanics" or the linkage that tied my poor self-esteem to my depression (I felt it, of course – I just could never "see" how the two were associated). But when my depression finally lifted, my self-esteem came forth and my self-perception normalized very quickly with a little effort on my part. I began to feel better about myself, almost immediately, as if a distorting filter had been removed from my eyes, which allowed me to see myself more as others saw me – more as I really was. To this day, I am still puzzled by the psycho-physiological connection between depression and lowered self-esteem, but the connection is real, and it is unmistakable.

I have not been depressed a single day since then. Not one.

I am happy now. I admit that I do not always feel fulfilled, but I am happy, and, though I feel sadness and frustrations and have disappointments just like anyone else, they are fleeting, and my happiness always returns because I am genuinely anchored by the five elements of the formula: *Purpose, Courage, Emotional Balance, Kindness & Related Ethics, and Self-Acceptance.*

Chapter 24

Self-Help

As you know, there are hundreds, if not thousands, of self-help books sold every year, on all sorts of topics. Some people buy them because they are moderately curious about learning new things, some are looking to save money by buying a book instead of seeking out a professional in whatever area they are interested in, and some might be looking to help someone else with a problem, but many (I suspect most) self-help book buyers are looking for a quick fix to be had in the privacy of their own home – a silver bullet in the form of written advice for a relatively small fee. And, I'm okay with that. In fact, I'm an *advocate* of it. I believe in the concept of self-help, and I believe it can work for just about anyone, which is one of the reasons I wrote this book. Words are powerful things and words become thoughts and philosophies and principles and methods and formulas, and these can become valuable guides to live by. But there's a catch. Well, not so much a catch as a condition. *You gotta do the work*. Self-help books *aren't* silver bullets that imbue a person with instantaneous wisdom. It doesn't take *a lot* of effort, in my opinion, but it does take some. It also takes a commitment to repetition.

When I was young, around the age of 16 or 17, as I recall, I decided that having a good vocabulary was a pretty good thing to have. I admired people that spoke and wrote well and knew words that painted a more nuanced picture than average, every-day words could. The more words a person knew, I observed, the more control they had of their conversations and speeches, and the more confident they were in the way in which they spoke. People with big vocabularies always seemed smarter to me, and I knew that to get that way, they had to have dedicated themselves to earnestly absorbing all those words, because, while intelligence might be genetic, an extensive vocabulary is *learned*. So, in setting out to improve my vocabulary, I told myself that one way to truly learn the meaning of words was to look them up in the dictionary while I was reading something (yes, young people, I was alive during the time of Webster's, hand-held, non-digital, non-phone-platform, hard-cover dictionary).

In the past, like most people reading a book, any time I came to a word I didn't know, I would scan for context for a few seconds in the lines above and below, then continue on, without really knowing the true definition. But, after I began my steadfast pursuit of a robust vocabulary, I made a pact with myself that I would stop and look up any word that I could not readily define. I did this fanatically for many, many years. And it worked. I didn't remember every word I looked up, but I remembered a lot of them. And, an even *bigger* impact on my vocabulary occurred when I wrote down the words and their abbreviated definitions on a piece of paper and *returned* to my list to remind myself of their definitions a second and third and fourth time. This extra effort in revisiting their meanings improved my retention by at least double, which allowed me to remember, long-term, probably 80% or more of the words I looked up. [And for those shaking your heads, yes, I know how "nerdy" this is because the few friends that I told about this have made fun of me relentlessly ever since.] The same is true with self-help material. You might remember some of it when you first read it, but if you really want it to stick – to truly imprint in your mind – you have to come back to it more than once.

Self-help and self-study is great. It really is. Buy all the books and magazines you can afford in order to try to improve your mind and your life – I am all for it. But when you read that book, magazine, one of these chapters, or some other self-help material, do two things and I guarantee it will make a very big difference: 1) Take time to highlight the concepts and passages that you feel are most important, and then 2) leave the material out in plain sight so that you will be prompted to come back to it again. Philosophies, principles, insights, and other profundities do not favor the man or woman on a drive-by, as it were. No, self-help wisdoms only bind to those willing to stop and learn and to revisit their studies several times more. When you do this, you will quickly come to see the difference between the ability to recall and the ability to *know*. True learning and behavioral change, no matter the area involved – life philosophies, fitness routines, leadership practices, welding, yoga, or vocabulary words – come about only after application and repetition – and all it takes is a little effort and the dedication to make it a habit.

> *Ultimately, the greatest help is self-help.*[35]
>
> – Bruce Lee

Chapter 25

Character and Kids

The little world of childhood with its familiar surroundings is a model of the greater world. The more intensively the family has stamped its character upon the child, the more it will tend to feel and see its miniature world again in the bigger world of adult life.[36]

– Carl Jung

I was talking to my good friend Joe (the same Joe as from the *Introduction*), and because he likes to read many of the things I write, I asked him if there were any topics he would like to suggest. He said that as a father of two young sons and a coach for several youth sports teams, he most likes to read topics that have to do with virtues. He said he likes to incorporate the principles of virtue in his discussions with his children and with the kids he interacts with as a coach, so he said he would really like to see something on "character." I'm not sure there is any topic more important in the context of mentoring our youth in how to be excellent humans, so I wrote this with parents, coaches, teachers, and other mentors in mind. A tip of the hat to my friend: *Thank you, Joe.*

Because of its indisputable importance, character has been widely written about for many hundreds of years. The number of quotations on the subject is immense, and I have no reason to think that what I have to say here will be any more poignant than anything that has been written or spoken before me – in fact, I am sure it won't be. But one thing that I have learned from talking to people about such things for many years is that sometimes saying it *differently*, from a different angle, using specifically chosen words, or using a very specific analogy, for example, can make the difference between something that is remembered and something that isn't. That said, these are the ways in which I think about character:

What it is

- Character is what keeps a person in harmony with virtue. It is the living result of your daily decisions to listen to or ignore your conscience
- Character is the ethical identity of an individual, and a person's identity is made up of a foundation and framework built by that person's choice of noble and honorable traits
- Character is constructed over time. Each moral and ethical decision we make either *adds* a stone or *removes* one from the structure. Good decisions are the essence of good character
- Reputation is the *messaging* that results from one's projected character. The goal, of course, is for the "advertising" to be congruent with the actual product. When a person lives up to his reputation, *there* is his character
- In the *world*, the law is the set of rules we apply to maintain a fair, reasonable, and just society. In a *person*, one's character is also a set of rules – rules of self-governance – that serve to make the *individual* reasonable, fair, and just

What it does

- Character does the right thing
- Character stands up for the right thing. Character is the thing that sometimes makes for a "majority of one" *("...any man more right than his neighbors constitutes a majority of one..."*[37] – Thoreau)
- Character tells the truth even when the truth hurts the teller
- Character champions justice and stops injustice
- Character takes action and does not stay silent
- Character admits fault and takes the blame
- Character puts others first, whenever possible
- Character does *good* for the sake of it

What it causes

- Character causes people to listen
- Character causes people to believe
- Character inspires others
- Character causes people to have courage and hope
- Character causes a feeling of accountability, even and *especially* when you are accountable to no one but yourself
- Character causes faith in humankind
- Character causes people to emulate it

What it earns

- Respect
- Loyalty
- Admiration
- Trust
- Peace of mind
- Benefit of the doubt
- Goodwill

Character, more than by anything else, is formed by the *decisions* we make regarding what we stand for and the *decisions* we make in support of those things. In teaching our children about this personal and crucial concept of identity-building, it is imperative that we stress this aspect above all. Yes, our character is in many respects *who* and *what* we are, but before this is so, our character is formed by what we *do.* William Durant said, *"Excellence is an art won by training and habituation. We do not act rightly because we have virtue or excellence, but we rather have those because we have acted rightly. We are what we repeatedly do. Excellence, then, is not an act but a habit."*[38] Character is the very same.

One does not achieve good character by doing the right thing on Tuesday. One achieves character by doing the right thing on *all*

Tuesdays and all days in between. Character is not perfection, of course, so one can stumble now and then without tragedy, but character is about integrity and integrity is about consistency, which is about a sincere *commitment* to one's values. And, commitment, just like these other values, is another construct that requires action – daily and consistent action in pursuit of virtuous and honorable living, which never loses its value.

For those of you that may say, "Well, gee, that's all well and good with your big-time philosophizing about how we should all teach our kids about it, but how 'bout now you give us something we can use – *now*, why don't you give us something we can actually tell the kids in plain English…," this part is for you:

Character is –

- When your Mom or Dad makes a mistake that initially upsets you but you forgive them because a mistake is a mistake, and you know it isn't personal and it wasn't intentional
- When you see that your Dad accidentally gave you $10 more than he gave your brother and you bring the error to his attention
- When the coach yells at "82" for jumping off-sides in football practice, when it was really you (88), and you make sure to take the blame
- When everyone else in class is going along with James who is teasing Keith, but you grab Keith and walk away from the crowd with him, even though you are now getting teased yourself
- When the other team wins and you tell them "good game" and you do your best to really mean it, even though no one likes to lose
- When you have "the right" to hit your brother back because "he started it," but you don't because you know that two wrongs *don't* make a right
- When your Dad asks you to help your Mom with the groceries and you do it without complaining because you respect your Dad, and your Mom (whom you respect as well) needs the help

- When your best friend wins an award that you also competed for, and even though you may wish it were you, you give her a hug and let her know that you are happy for her
- When the other team is cheating and is probably going to win, but instead of cheating as well, which you also have the opportunity to do, you choose to play honest – because that's the right thing to do
- When the neighbor, Mr. Miller, gets some of his tools stolen and you know who did it, and even though you will be called a "rat" by some of the kids you know, you speak up and tell what you know, because it isn't fair that Mr. Miller should lose his property just because you are worried about being called names
- When everyone at school has been talking about how much they don't like one of the "mean" teachers because she gives a lot of low grades, but you defend her by saying that "she isn't mean – she just expects you to study and do your work, and when you do, you will get a good grade"
- When you are at the grocery store and someone has left a grocery cart out in the parking lot and instead of saying, "It's not my job to put it in the rack," you go get it and place it in the cart rack just because it's a nice thing to do for people trying to park *and* for the people that work at the store
- When you hit the car next to you with your car door and chip the paint, even though your Dad *just told you to be careful* opening the door, and you tell your Dad you did it – even though he is going to be mad, and even though you could get away with it – because it *was* your fault and it's only fair that you let the owner of the other car know what happened
- When one of your teammates wants to play a joke on one of the other players on your team that tends to get picked on… the joke is funny but kind of mean and you know the boy will be very embarrassed and hurt by it, so not only do you tell your teammate you aren't going to participate but you also tell the boy to beware so that he can avoid the prank
- When you are doing sit-ups or push-ups and you do them by yourself just as correctly as when the coach is watching

- When the boy that most of the other girls think is "gross" says hi to you in the hallway and you say hi back, even though you know your girlfriends are going to tease you. Because being kind is always the right thing to do
- When the teacher, due to a miscalculation, gives you a score of 92 on your math test, when your score should've been an 87, and you tell the teacher about the mistake, even though this will drop you from an "A" to a "B"
- When you get asked to go to a party by a good friend of yours (Thomas) on the same Friday night that you have already committed to going to a movie with a friend you are not quite as close to (Jack), so you tell Thomas that you are very sorry but you cannot go. Because character is about honoring our commitments
- When you strike out, you calmly walk away and quietly put your bat and helmet in their place in the dugout and you cheer on the next teammate up to bat. Because striking out doesn't make you a failure and because being a good sport and striking out with grace shows character
- When you donate to a charity at school or church or in the neighborhood, even though you won't get any "credit" for it. Because helping those less fortunate than you is always the right thing to do
- When you are working at a job where you are paid by the hour and the boss leaves 20 minutes before quitting time and won't be back, and you stay all the way to the end and work, even though several other employees left right after the boss did

Character is doing the right thing *because* it's the right thing. Because it is good and honest and helpful and kind and true.

Chapter 26

Leaders and Guilt

What a powerful force is guilt. What a mysterious phenomenon…

Almost everyone has a working conscience. Those who do often allow guilt to influence their thoughts, feelings, and behaviors to varying degrees. While I'm sure most people would agree that the conscience that produces guilt is an innate psychological construct, the *proportions* to which one's guilt rises in various situations is very much molded by one's environment and how guilt was either fostered or minimized by parents and other close relationships. So, while 99% of us feel guilt at times, there are widely varying *degrees* of guilt in people – it just depends on the combination of the conscience you were born with, how you were taught, and how you choose to respond given whatever combination of variables apply to you.

As with most things, I am relatively sure there is a normal distribution across populations (the bell curve) when it comes to guilt – a big middle ground and two sides of extremes. What I want to talk about here, however, are the two types of guilt and the benefits and detriments of guilt, in general, and guilt as it relates to the job of leaders, whether you are a supervisor, parent, or some other form of mentor or guide.

I have always believed guilt to be a good thing – *mostly*. It's a back-up system of sorts for those times when one's character and integrity aren't fully engaged. If we allow it to, guilt can help keep us honest. It's our moral compass, as they say, and it works very well when we let it work free of rationalization and justification.

When you feel the poke of guilt, it is usually a good idea to listen. Attempting to ignore it or suppress it only works temporarily, anyway, as it will continue to poke at you until you relieve yourself of it by doing whatever it is that rectifies the situation. Yes, guilt is a good thing, mostly, I believe, because it is an early warning system, a behavior-modification force, and it can prevent tragedy. Sometimes, though, guilt does an odd thing. Sometimes, it arises at times when it *doesn't* really make sense. For example, *survivor's guilt* is one of those times when people have no logical reason to feel guilty, but they still do. There is 1) righteous guilt – guilt that we *should* feel if our conscience is in good working order – and 2) *irrational* or *false guilt* (like survivor's guilt), which is guilt we feel that isn't particularly logical and that we really don't deserve to feel. False guilt isn't "bad," per se, but it is wrong-headed and without foundation, and though it is spontaneous and unintentionally misguided, it does cause problems.

Hurting people's feelings makes most of us feel bad. When we see or find out that someone has been hurt because of something we have said or done, we tend to feel bad for *them* and bad *about* ourselves – we feel regret/remorse and often guilt. But what if what we said *needed* to be said? What if a child or an employee of ours needed to be told that their conduct or performance disappointed us? Why should we feel guilty about that? If we were righteous in saying it and we said it appropriately, what is there to feel guilty about?

Sometimes, as parents, coaches, supervisors, etc., we must say things that hurt the other person. That isn't our intent, but that's the result. But did we truly *cause* that hurt, or was it caused by the person's behavior and their *response* to being confronted? Just because we may *precipitate* hurt feelings through our admonishments and corrections does not mean we are guilty of any offense. In fact, the opposite is often true. Regret/remorse and compassion and guilt often mix together to *feel* like one emotion, but they are distinct emotions that should be differentiated so that we don't confuse regret/remorse and compassion for guilt. Remorse and compassion are *branches* of the conscience and because they are connected to it, it often feels like we should be acting the same way toward them as we do toward guilt – but this does not fit.

If we have a student, an employee, or a child, for example, that is not doing what they should be doing, and we decide that we need to talk to them about it, we can very easily anticipate that they are going to be hurt or angry or both. When we fail to treat regret/remorse and compassion differently than we do righteous guilt, we have the tendency to hesitate or avoid saying the things that we need to say. When we see someone upset, we want to stop the hurt. If our comments "caused" the hurt, then ceasing the comments will stop it, which is good, we tell ourselves, because hurting others is bad (see how easy it is to lose our way when we fail to separate guilt from regret/remorse?). Because you are a good human with a conscience, you have compassion, and that compassion makes you feel that the situation was regrettable. Naturally, when someone has been hurt, the situation *is* regrettable, but in doing the right thing, you should not be compelled to feel *remorse* – the two *are* different.

When, as a leader/mentor, you have to say difficult things, ask yourself these questions: Do these things need to be said? Is the content of the statements fair and accurate? Did I *cause* the need for these things to be said? If the answers are *Yes, Yes,* and *No,* then you should proceed. If a feeling of "guilt" comes over you as you anticipate the meeting, ask yourself if what you are feeling is not actually a combination of compassion *and* a general aversion to conflict. *Yes, feelings will be hurt,* but does this warrant guilt? *Absolutely not.* And because feelings will most likely be hurt, does this mean compassion should not be applied? Well, yes and no. A sense of compassion should definitely not forestall the meeting, but it can and should still be applied *in* the meeting. In this same vein, many times what keeps us from doing things that will cause discomfort in others gets labeled as guilt, which confuses us and dissuades us from taking rightful and righteous action. To correct ourselves, what we must do is become more attuned to our *true* feelings and motivations so that guilt emerges only when it is appropriate; otherwise, we allow *false* guilt to cloud our judgment and to prevent us from doing what is right in our role as leaders. To withhold the truth from those we are responsible for is to withhold from them an opportunity for personal growth and greater happiness. And helping others to be happy is another wonderful way for us to feel happy ourselves.

> *When we don't allow others to suffer the consequences of their actions, we cripple them emotionally. We deprive them of the ability to learn from their mistakes. We also take away their ability to overcome their problems and change their life for the better.*[39]
> – Randi G. Fine

Chapter 27

The Only Thing You Can Be

There are many philosophies that I have employed in my life over the years, many ideas and principles that I have done my best (more often than not) to follow that have helped me to be happier, wiser (allegedly, arguably), more at peace, more confident, and so on, and I have written about many of these in this book. And one of these philosophies that I was fortunate enough to come by at a relatively young age was this one: That having the courage to be myself is important to my overall sense of happiness. I'm not claiming to have always been so inclined – I dabbled in various personas and facets of various "personalities" just like most insecure, young people do, but, ultimately, I knew that learning to be comfortable with who I am would be very important to my overall contentment and self-acceptance. Of course, learning to be myself, to becoming "comfortable in my own skin," as they say, doesn't mean I *became* who I am at 37, for example, and that was that. What I mean by learning to be myself is being true to my beliefs and preferences and feelings to the degree that I did not necessarily feel compelled to conform to those of others. I know who I am, what I believe and why, and though I do often listen to others and learn from them, the decisions I make about what being *me* is are based on the influences of my own ethics and standards and not on society's or some other group or individual.

In my junior high school, all the boys wore *Levis* – except for a small group that wore *Wranglers*. I thought *Wranglers* looked good in a different way than did *Levis*, and girls often seemed to like the boys that wore *Wranglers*, but only the "cowboys" wore them, and they were only a very small percentage of the school. None of the *non*-cowboys ever wore *Wranglers*, but I really wanted to try them to see if they would look good on me, too, so I bought a pair, got them home, washed them, and tried them on in my room. *I looked like a dufus. Wranglers,* generally speaking, look best on people with more... *gluteals,* shall we say, and bigger legs. I weighed about 85 pounds in those days, so while I found some that fit me in length (barely), they looked horribly over-sized and slouchy. I *knew* I wasn't a *Wranglers* guy before I even went to the store, but because I was trying to be something I wasn't, I gave them a shot. *It did not work out.*

What I learned from this teenage moment was several very important things: 1) When you know you're not a *Wranglers* guy, don't try to be one; 2) Trying to pull off something that isn't you, makes you look like a phony; 3) Trying to be someone *else* is a waste of money; 4) I looked just fine as a *Levis* guy; 5) and, being *myself* is much simpler and a lot more comfortable than trying to be someone else.

Here's the beauty of this philosophy: Being yourself is the very easiest thing there is to be *and* the most honest *and* the most attractive, which means it is also the most effective (or *efficacious*, if I were trying to be "fancy" and something I am not) – that is to say, *if* we have the courage to be or become the person we *really* want to be. And therein lies "the rub," as they say. The person we really want to be and the person we *say* we want to be or *are posing as* are often very different, and that difference is due to various and sundry ulterior motives. And while these motives come in the form of all sorts of de-motivations and anxieties and excuses and psychological infirmities, they all have just one thing in common: the lack of courage to pursue *full-time realness.* Yes, I know that is not a very eloquent way of putting it, but that's exactly what it is.

As I have grown older, I have had other moments of insecurity-based, persona experimentation, of course, similar to the *Wranglers* incident, but they have been fewer and fewer over the years. This is so because of how "out-of-sorts" they made me feel, how awkward and incongruent these instances felt. For the most part, especially in my older adulthood, I have been true to myself, and being such has allowed me to be happy. When people talk about someone being "very natural," it's because that person is comfortable with the way they speak and act and think out loud. I have never met anyone *anywhere* who doesn't appreciate the qualities of sincerity and realness. And no matter who you are, *real* is always a good look.

If you don't want light green to be "your color," even though your Mother says that's your color, that's fine – don't claim it. Just make sure you're choosing another color for the right reasons (you know, instead of because you don't like light green because your Mother *does* like it). If you want to be an artist, even though your family wants you to be an engineer, stick to what *you* want to be. You won't be happy if you don't. Why let peer, family, or some other sub-cultural pressure co-opt you into doing something you don't really want to do? As with most things, if your heart isn't in it, you're going to be miserable.

As long as being yourself is a *good* thing, in the sense that it is logical and reasonable and merely a matter of preference (vs. ethics and morals), then *always* be yourself. If there are ten people in a room, all of whom like "Southern Rock," and they ask you who your favorite band is, why pretend it's the *Allman Brothers Band*, when you really like *Prince*? What do you gain? A bit more momentary acceptance, a cosmetic sense of camaraderie, an air of comfortability you didn't have before, or a slightly augmented sense of security? All of these are temporary and ultimately meaningless. On the other hand, what do you lose? Even though it's just a fib about music, do you not forfeit some integrity? Do you not lose a little self-respect in knowing that you didn't have the courage to admit to liking *His Royal Badness/The Purple One/His Funkiness*? Do you not lose *their* respect, should they find out later you were just trying to fit in for some trivial personal gain? The losses are much greater than the gains, I assure you.

Being yourself as a child, a teenager, and even a young adult, can be difficult. It really can. It *does* take courage, sometimes, to be whom you want to be, given how judgmental and petty our society can be. But being true to yourself is *much* easier than faking it. It also gets easier the more you do it. Courage *begets* courage. By the time you are an older adult, being yourself should be second nature (although I am aware that it is not much easier for some at 45 than at 25). But the point is, it *should* be. And *can* be, if we decide we are going to go with what feels right, with what feels like the best fit – with what feels *real*.

Being yourself is always the easiest thing you can be, and it is certainly the *best* thing. And if you don't want to take my word for it, just ask someone who isn't. It will be written all over them (which is how you will know to ask). *Be yourself.* It *is* the easiest thing you can be, and the truth is, in the end, it's really the *only* thing you can be.

> *You don't have to change who you are; you have*
> *to become more of who you are.*[40]
>
> – Sally Hogshead

Chapter 28

Grief and Healing

Grief is an abysmal, heavy, usurping emotion. I know of nothing worse. It is the most difficult to endure and the emotion that takes the longest to reset to "normal." It is sadness, anguish, and loneliness wrapped into one overwhelming emotion that punches us in the gut, taking our wind and spirit away, often in an instant. Grief is the hardest emotion there is. But, there is hope, and there is peace that will come in time.

Many books have been written on the subject of grief. *Understandably so.* I read several of these books during the time I was training to be a counselor many years ago, and while I vaguely recall that these books were insightful and accurate in their evaluations of grief and how to cope with it, I also found the academic perspective (which is perfectly understandable in a book of psychology) to be less satisfying than I had hoped. My objective in this chapter is to bring to this topic less theory and hopefully a little more practical philosophy and understanding.

As I think of it, the crux of it all may very well be this: The suddenness and gravity and finality of death is an unfairly disproportionate outcome in comparison to the wonderment and fullness and splendor that is/was life. Death, as a conclusion to life, is analogous to a punishment not fitting the crime. Death is simply too much – it is *overkill*. The agonizing pain of loss feels to be greater – especially in the beginning of our mourning – than is commensurate with the magnitude of life. It feels like death has taken more than its share. How can so much beautiful animation, depth, complexity, and sheer time on this earth be concluded by something as sterile, instantaneous, and final as death? The answer is that it can't be – not fairly, I mean. It is a conclusion that simply does not equal all the life that has preceded it.

145

For those of you who may be in the midst of grief at this moment, I would like for you to know that my intent in analyzing it like this is to acknowledge that the unfairness that you may be feeling is completely understandable – the fact that you feel such a chasmic disparity between life and death is perfectly reasonable – *more* than reasonable. Death is simply not fair.

And, if you are in the midst of grief, I will not presume this to be the best time to discuss the "grieving process" – that term is so cold and void of feeling. There is a time, of course, to address the path to healing, but for now, perhaps it is premature. I can certainly understand if that is how you feel. And if that is the case, all that I know to offer you right now is patience, understanding, and the hope of peace. Mourning is very personal and individual. Each person has their own clock – *as it should be*. There will come a time, soon enough, when you will engage "the process" and you will be ready to climb that difficult peak. Hopefully, you will know when that time is – it could be tomorrow, or it could be months from now. Until that time, regardless of when it is, please know that while those around you may not be able to understand *exactly* what you are going through, we are trying hard to understand as best we can. We want to be there for you in whatever ways you need – but most of all, we wish for you healing and peace of mind.

The *healing* part of grief is just as personal as the mourning itself, if not more so. Each person, ultimately, must do so within their own minds – alone. Yes, there will be people around to support you – sometimes many – but, ultimately, all mourning is borne individually, no matter how much emotional support there may be from others. That's what makes it so difficult. As much as others may want to relieve you of the weight of bereavement, they can remove only a percentage of the immensity with which that grief weighs us down. Grief is intense and pervasive and despairing, and it seems like it will never end. And in some ways, I think most would say, it really does *not* end – it only diminishes in intensity. Undoubtedly, the intensity of the pain does decrease over time, but it never goes away completely – it is like a train that becomes smaller and smaller as it moves solemnly away in the distance, but it is a train that never quite reaches its destination. There *is* hope in grief and in healing, but that hope is very much dependent on time. It is also dependent on perspective.

For those of you at any stage of grieving, you will encounter people who mean well, of course, but who do not and cannot fully understand what you are feeling and who, therefore, sometimes say what often feels like the wrong thing. People tend to want to rush those in mourning because they want them to feel better as soon as possible. What people do not often understand, unfortunately, is that mourning has its own clock, and that that clock runs at a different pace for each individual, which is why this is such a personal emotion and a personal process. And though the sadness may never go away completely, it is possible, in time, to feel that one has finally healed. It may take a very *long* time, but healing *does* occur. Sometimes, time alone does it, but most of the time, true healing requires an additional element, which is where perspective comes in.

Healing is not about "moving on," "learning to forget," or "deciding not to be sad anymore." These things are often stated, but to be frank, they are misguided, no matter how innocently they might be uttered. Healing is about learning to put the loss in perspective. It is very much about acceptance and reason and healthy coping skills. Learning to hurt less over the loss of a loved one does not mean you have forgotten the one you lost. It does not mean you have moved on, and it does not mean your loved one is any less important to you because you are learning to heal. Healing simply means that you have found logical and healthy ways to cope with your grief and in a manner that allows you to function somewhat better than the day before. While suffering may feel like a way in which we can pay tribute to those we have lost, it is a form of tribute that we are often reluctant to conclude – which is perfectly understandable – but which is usually unhealthy and sometimes even harmful.

Many people that perceive suffering in this way – as a form of tribute – never conclude their suffering because to do so in their minds would be to conclude the tribute, which they are disinclined to do. In my opinion, *love*, not suffering, is the greatest tribute there is, and we can carry on our love for those we have lost without sacrificing our own peace of mind or mental health. For instance, remembrance is love;

wanting for yourself that which they would also want for you is love (being happy!); talking to them quietly or praying for them is love; conducting yourself in a way that would make them proud is love. *All of these* are love, and though there may be some heartache involved, especially in the beginning, one need not suffer to do these things or to express love in any other way. And one certainly need not feel guilty that healing is taking place. One should not feel guilty that one's grief is subsiding. Less pain does not equal less love or less remembrance. It simply does not.

If you are in the midst of grieving, please know that the intensity of the pain you feel *will* pass. Time truly does heal. It will not wipe out the pain completely and it will not do so quickly, but there is hope of better days for all who mourn. For those of you at a stage in the process where you are able to at least *conceive* of there being hope of some relief in time, please remember that "getting better" is not about learning to care less. It is simply a natural process afforded by time and, for those willing to try, by a healthy perspective.

We were not meant to be in a state of perpetual suffering. We have lives to live and people to take care of, and while it feels as though there is no fairness in the loss of a loved one, we are not given a choice in these matters, and when choice is taken from us, often the best perspective is a combination of acceptance and reason – acceptance that death is a very sad and difficult part of life (but a part nonetheless) and that it is unreasonable not to learn to accept it. This is a difficult perspective to embrace in the midst of grief, but it is a healthy and productive one. We all have a clock and each clock runs at a different speed. Take your time, but be kind to yourself and do your best to keep healing in the back of your mind. Healing isn't forgetting – it's just healing.

She was no longer wrestling with the grief, but could sit down with it as a lasting companion and make it a sharer in her thoughts.[41]
– George Eliot

Hope smiles from the threshold of the year to come,
whispering 'it will be happier'...[42]

– Alfred Lord Tennyson

Chapter 29

Depression, Suicide, and Suicide Prevention

Before we begin, I want to be clear that none of the information or statements on depression should be construed as medical or any other form of professional advice. These are general statements intended to be educational and to familiarize you in a very general sense with what depression looks like and feels like and how best to approach it, therapeutically. If you think you may be suffering from depression, you should contact a licensed counselor, psychiatrist, and/or your physician.

Depression affects approximately 10% of the female population and approximately 5% of the male population (though the percentage is believed to be higher, particularly in males, due to under-reporting) and is suffered along a spectrum – that is, some depression is mild, some is moderate, and some is severe. There are two main categories of depression: "situational" and "clinical." Situational depression is triggered by an event such as a break-up or a loss and is usually relatively short-lived. Clinical depression or "major depressive disorder" is a more severe form of depression, often has a genetic and/or biochemical component, and very often lasts longer than depression resulting from a specific event or series of events.

Symptoms common to both types of depression can include the following –

- Depressed mood or sustained irritability
- Reduced interest or feeling no pleasure in activities
- Decrease or increase in appetite
- Decrease or increase in desire or ability to sleep
- Loss of energy, listlessness
- Trouble concentrating or making decisions
- Feelings of worthlessness, hopelessness

- Recurrent thoughts of death or suicide

Situational depression *can* go away on its own, but it often does not without assistance. Clinical depression is more severe and is much less likely to dissipate on its own. Depression is *not* extreme sadness. It is a completely different state of mind unto itself that can last for years, if left untreated.

Both forms of depression can very often be treated successfully with medication and/or counseling, and medication can be initiated by your primary care physician, or an OBGYN, for example. Yes, psychiatrists can prescribe medications for depression, as they are MDs and DOs trained in mental health treatment, but a person is not required to see a psychiatrist in order to begin a trial of medication(s) for depression. I am not advocating for or against psychiatrists. I am merely stating that one can inquire with their general practitioner (GP) just as easily. In my experience with many client-employees over the years, GPs and OBGYNs are glad to discuss relevant medications for depression and prescribe them routinely when appropriate. The medications commonly prescribed for depression are quite effective with relatively low-level side effects. Many, if not most doctors, will also recommend "talk therapy" (counseling) as a supplement/complement to medication. Statistically, the combination of counseling *and* medication in clinical depression is more successful than either counseling or medication, singularly.

Depression is debilitating and often gets worse, so it is wise to address it as soon as you think you may have it. You are more likely to use a counselor/therapist if they are conveniently located near your home or work, so when you look them up online, I recommend you look primarily for what they specialize in to match with your needs and that you look for one that will be near your daily routes. Counselors are no different than doctors or barbers/hair stylists or mechanics in that sometimes it takes a few tries before you find one you like, that *gets* you, that you trust and relate to.

Counselors or psychotherapists, generally speaking, come in these categories of education (there are other degrees you will see on your insurance company's list of mental health providers and on the internet, but these are the primary ones):

- Psychiatrists are MDs or DOs who specialize in the diagnosis and treatment of mental illness
- PhDs are clinical psychologists with backgrounds heavy in clinical research, as well as in counseling
- PsyDs are psychologists whose education focused primarily on counseling
- LSMFTs are licensed marriage and family therapists, who work primarily with couples and/or families on issues within the family
- MSWs or LCSWs are counselors with a Master's degree in social work, their specialty, generally speaking, being primarily community, agency-based counseling, though not necessarily
- Licensed Professional Counselors (LPCs) are Master's level counselors who trained almost exclusively in counseling and completed a lengthy practicum first in school and again in their initial training as a professional

In my opinion, the best way to choose a counselor is to meet them. Natural ability and skill are far more important than the degree on the wall. Some counselors are naturally gifted, but many are not. The only way to know is to schedule an appointment and see if you mesh.

Improving mental health, just like physical health, requires action. Some people are born with low body fat and a predisposition for physical fitness, but most have to work at it. The same is true for mental health. We all know people that were born happy and care-free – but a lot of people were not. Life can be hard. We are not all bestowed with the same genetic gifts in physical health or in mental health. If you want to get fit – whatever kind of fit we are talking about – you have to take charge of your situation, and each day is a new opportunity to do so.

Whatever the origins of depression and despondency may be in someone's life, suicide is about the loss of hope. I think about this topic a lot and decided to strip away all the platitudes and the academics we see and hear about suicide and distill the discussion into the simplest message possible.

People who consider taking their life by suicide or people who actually die by suicide, at that particular moment in time, feel that all hope is gone. They hurt so badly and feel so hopeless that the only solution they can think of is ending the pain permanently. Obviously, therefore, the best way to help someone, whether you are a counselor, a Mom/Dad, a friend, or the person that just happens to notice the man or woman crying at the airport, is to help them to feel hope. You don't have to know anything about psychology or depression to render aid in the form of hope. And much of the time, *most* of the time, for those in need, the most important piece of evidence that there *is* still hope is seeing/feeling that someone cares.

Not everyone is equipped in the long-term to help people that are suicidal. *That's OK.* It is. But most everyone is equipped to show someone – even a stranger – that you care. If you are not the person that is best prepared to help someone with their depression, but you are caring and concerned enough to say something, that's all you have to do. Just say enough to make a connection. Tell the person you may not be able to understand their troubles perfectly, but you care and want to help them.

Sincere, caring, kind people can often make a connection in mere seconds, and, sometimes, that's all that is needed to decrease a percentage of that person's sense of hopelessness. Humanity and compassion are powerful things. They are at the top of my list for suicide prevention. If you see someone in need, show them you care. All you have to do is be human and let them see your compassion. Once they have cause to believe there is a reason to go on one more day, do your best to get them to a physician and/or a counselor. Many times, that's all it takes to help someone get back on their feet.

Obviously, the topic of suicide runs much deeper than what is discussed in this short chapter. There is an infinite array of circumstances in the lives of those who are suicidal, many levels of dejection, anomalies, and many things that can go wrong, but, generally speaking, people in despair need a reason to feel hope, and most anyone can bring hope to someone with as little as a caring hand on the shoulder and a quiet voice of concern. Sometimes, that anyone is the person that notices, at some arbitrary moment in time, the look of deep sadness or loss on another's face. Sometimes, that anyone may be sitting, or walking, or living a short distance away from the someone that is desperate for a break in the clouds. Never assume less of your position or of your ability to help, because sometimes that anyone is you.

The National Suicide Prevention Lifeline number for 24/7 crisis help is 1-800-273-8255 (TALK), which is also now accessible by dialing 988.

Chapter 30

Hard Times

Hard times, in one form or another, will befall most of us in our lifetime. Some will go through *many* hard times and some only a few, but *very* few of us will get through this life unscathed by pain, tragedy, or some relatively prolonged adversity. Life is often very difficult. And it can be very difficult through no fault of our own. Many times, it *is* of our own doing, but many times it is not, and it is during these times that the way in which we choose to react to these times determines the level of our unhappiness and how quickly we choose to allow happiness to return to us. Happiness is a state of mind. A state of *being*. And though the random pitfalls of life can very easily affect our happiness, in the long-term, our happiness is more often affected by choice than by circumstance.

I know people that have been severely injured, that have terminal cancer, that have gotten divorced, lost jobs, filed bankruptcy, lost loved ones, and suffered many other disheartening tragedies. What makes one person rise above the pain and another, under equal circumstances, remain dejected and dismayed is an attitude of emotional resilience, of optimism, of courage, and of determination. All of these are a matter of *choice*. Just as are surrender, pessimism, fear, and self-pity. I am not for one second implying that being happy during hard times is easy. What I am saying is that allowing hard times to crush your spirit and steal your happiness is a decision one makes. My hope for anyone going through hard times is that they will choose to conquer the hard times, to look toward the horizon, and with each new day decide that happiness, in time, can and will be recaptured. But it *is* a decision.

Hope is everything. Without it, we can make no progress, so when hope is gone, we cannot simply wait for it to return. It just doesn't work that way. Hope is not sent by the cosmos, controlled by some mysterious external source. Hope is human. It is ours, and it is within our control, so when things seem hopeless, we have two choices: to concede that the world is bigger and tougher than we are, or we can choose to *create* hope, to *will* it into being. Hope is human, and it is ours to control.

When someone tells me that they are in a "hopeless" situation, there are several thoughts that immediately come to my mind. My first thought is that *this is heart-breaking and I want to help.* My second thought is that *I refuse to accept that anything is hopeless, so let's work through this because hopelessness is just a temporary illusion, a perspective that can be changed as long as you are determined to change it;* and, lastly, *Is hopelessness really an option?*

If you look for good people in the world, you will find them. If you look for *bad* people, you will find them, too. Whatever you are looking for in this life, you will find – it all depends on what you decide to look for. And hope is the very same. I know that hope is very difficult to hang onto during hard times. I struggled for 22 years – every *day* of those 22 years. And every day, I chose not to surrender. Hopelessness was *never* an option for me because I chose against it. I am not suggesting that during that time I was always optimistic. I absolutely was not. But I never gave up, laid down, or submitted to the mirage of hopelessness. As bad as I felt, as inescapable as was my depression, I chose to have hope. Many days I hung onto little more than a frayed and single strand of it, but it was just enough of a lifeline to keep me going.

Hard times are almost inevitable. We can choose to work through them with the encouragement of self-generated hope, or we can accept defeat and watch our lives slip away into ruin. These are our two options, and one of these isn't really much of an option at all. So, choose hope. The other choice – hopelessness – just doesn't work out.

We must accept finite disappointment, but never lose infinite hope.[43]
– Martin Luther King, Jr.

Chapter 31

The Benefits of Adversity

Although we are very social creatures and are with co-workers, friends, and family much of the day, other portions of the day are solitary to varying degrees of time, depending on one's living arrangements and general social preferences. Whether you are a person who doesn't mind being alone very much or someone who doesn't like it at all, there are always going to be times when you are forced to be alone with nothing more than your own thoughts. And, as with many other aspects of our human personalities, how comfortable you are being alone is dictated by two things: genetics and environment (learning/conditioning). Early on in our development, most of us heard from our parents in many areas that *"you need to learn to do this on your own."* Some of us take to this philosophy like ducks to water; others, naturally, are less enthusiastic and require a bit more convincing. Regardless of where one falls on this spectrum, the point is that the theme of independence and self-reliance is one that is emphasized from a very early age, due to its inherent benefits.

Independence is good because it helps us manage our lives when there is no one else to help us. Being independent allows us to do things as a solitary human when another person is simply not around. We teach our kids this philosophy at an early age because we all know that no matter what topic we may be discussing, there will always be times *"when I won't be there to help you"* – therefore, we promote a spirit and a philosophy of independence so that when we *aren't* there, their progress and success won't be forestalled. Sure, we are a bit glad that they "need" us, but we should feel *most* comfortable when they don't, because, ultimately, independence and self-reliance equals safety, security, advancement, evolution, inner strength, and peace of mind.

Sometimes, in our evolutionary progressions as we get older, however, it seems to me that we tend to forget this philosophy of independence and lose sight of how important this philosophy is at *all* stages of our lives. Learning to be independent is not just learning to do things we have never done before – that's what it is in the beginning, mostly, yes – later, though, it is more often about learning to power through things on our own when no one but ourselves can get them done, even if someone else *were* standing there.

In the beginning of our development, becoming "independent" is mostly about physical and practical things, such as training wheels and flash cards and role modeling, which, of course, are all good things. As we get older and life gets tougher, however, being independent is defined more about emotional independence as it relates to overcoming *adversity*. Emotional independence, generally speaking, is what allows us to work out problems on our own instead of having to ask our parents for help, for example. Emotionally independent people deal with anxieties differently than those who aren't. Emotionally independent people generally search their stores of experience and wisdom for solutions to conflict. Those that aren't emotionally independent tend to begin looking for *comfort*. Sometimes that's in the form of simple avoidance and sometimes it is in the form of passing off the problem to someone else. Instead of trying to sort things out for themselves and facing up to the problem, they either walk away from it altogether or they start reaching for a rescue rope. Hopefully, you know that I am not criticizing people that ask for help or that ask for another's opinion – that would be the pinnacle of irony for a guy in my position – but there is a big difference between giving up or asking for help before one has tried to work it out for themselves first and asking for help as a last resort.

Life is hard sometimes, *often* even. And those that are best at navigating life are often those that have had many opportunities to experience life's myriad adversities. Who are the best fighters – those that have lost several times and learned to improve on their past mistakes, or those that have never lost? I'm sure we would all agree that 99% of the time, it is those that have lost and overcome. Adversity has a natural way of making us smarter, better, tougher, and wiser. Yet, most of us dislike conflict and adversity. This is logical enough, but one doesn't have to like adversity to reap its benefits.

I didn't like it the first time I had a flat tire away from home or the second time I got kicked in the guts doing martial arts or the third time

I tried to back a cattle trailer through a gate while people were watching. But each of these unpleasant events taught me something because I chose to push through and use that particular adversity to my advantage. I could've called for help, called a time out, and asked for someone else to do it, but in pushing through, in attempting to address the adversity first, on my own, I was able to turn adversity into greater experience and confidence, knowing that if these events occurred again, they would be more familiar, less intimidating, and less...*adverse*. Unfortunately, however, many times when adversity visits itself upon us, we look for the path of least resistance instead of using it as an opportunity to grow. I'm not saying that if your tire takes a nail, you shouldn't call your insurance and have the roadside crew come and tend to it while you wait safely off the road and out of traffic because by calling them you are passing up such a golden opportunity to learn how to change a tire on the tollway at 6:15 p.m. What I *am* saying is that adversity can be good, if you give it its due.

Counselors like for people to work out problems on their own whenever possible. Parents *should* want their children to work out problems on their own whenever possible. Bosses *should* want their managers to work out problems on their own whenever possible. Why? Because independence equals experience and experience equals growth and because *there's not always going to be someone there to help you.* You want to be mentally tough, at ease, at peace, un-anxious about life? View every occasion of conflict as an opportunity to learn something new, to get stronger, to add another layer of resilience to your psyche. How many times have we heard, *"What doesn't kill us makes us stronger"?* Well, it didn't become a platitude by not being true.

When adversity knocks at the door (or crashes into it, because sometimes that's what it does), I recommend doing your very best to try to work through it. That doesn't mean you can't ask for help – *of course, you can* – but you still have to go through the fire to get the benefit of the forge – steel does not become hardened without it. Setbacks, losses, upheavals, sadness, depression, and outright tragedies are going to happen – we have no choice in many of these. What we *do* have a choice in is using these experiences to get better and wiser and stronger *or*... ignoring them, patching over them, or passing them off to someone else to deal with. If we are going to have to deal with adversity anyway, why not get some value from it?

When someone asks for volunteers to do something that they have never done before, how many people do you think raise their hands? In my experience, maybe 1 out of 10. We like comfort. It's easy. Taking chances, feeling insecure over safe, feeling scared versus relaxed is not something we humans tend to seek out – it's rather counterintuitive to be frank. But, if you are looking to improve, looking to take your game up a notch, looking to go from okay to confident, from anxious to resilient, try to start looking at life like *Whac-a-Mole*, or, on the meaner side of things, like *saaaay*... a gladiator pit with intermittently charging tigers. But, whether moles or tigers, life is going to keep sending stuff to mess with you, so the best thing you can do is to stay in the fight so that you can get better at it. The more life battles you have, the better, as long as you are using them as learning experiences and not just things you can "ride around" without really resolving the conflict. The more moles and tigers you whack, the more proficient you become, and pretty soon, as with anything else, what used to be difficult becomes downright easy. Life really *does* get easier if your goal is to get better at it, and taking on challenges with courage and a spirit of independence is exactly what will help you get there. And when life becomes easier, *one becomes happier*. Oh, how I love it when things all come together...

Never to suffer would never to have been blessed.[44]
– Edgar Allen Poe

Adversity introduces a man to himself.[45]
– Albert Einstein

Chapter 32

Perseverance

At most of the places we go to work in this world, the concept of perseverance is a good philosophy. In most job situations, or even just in regular life where task-based activities arise, perseverance is a very good thing to apply, because perseverance is what often gets the job done. More specifically, it's what gets the *hard* jobs done. The truth is, the *easy* jobs tend to get done with just consistent, run-of-the-mill effort. It's the really difficult, time-sapping, tedious, highly complex, ugly jobs that require perseverance. And that's where some humans really shine.

Perseverance, tenacity, determination, fortitude, resolve, heart, work ethic, etc. – whatever nuance one prefers – are all very powerful tools. I think of perseverance as a "force multiplier," even as a sort of lever that makes hard work easier. There are people that say about a difficult job with a short deadline, *"Mmmmmm, that's going to be pretty tough by that date."* And then there are those that say, *"No problem – it'll be done by then."* That's commitment, determination, and pride – all things that make up what it is to persevere.

Perseverance does great things in those who apply it. Those who persevere accomplish almost everything they set out to accomplish. When they grow weary, they push on. When they feel that those around them may not be as dedicated, they push on. When the cause is righteous, regardless of any other factors that may impede or subtract from their efforts, *they push on.* Because that's what perseverance is: commitment, determination, and pride.

There are many, many instances in life in which *not* persevering or just plain quitting is pretty easy, and the consequences of such are not particularly tragic. Painting the inside of the garage, finishing your genealogy project, organizing the trunk of your car, and so on do not transform an otherwise well-led life into one of calamity if these jobs are not completed in a timely way. But other jobs – inspiring, disciplining, and leading our children, being an excellent employee, working to increase our knowledge and wisdom, achieving our true potential in life, improving ourselves as human beings are all things, I would argue, that we should persevere in. These missions, these causes are *righteous*. They matter. And when something matters, it only makes sense to persevere in order to ensure that the job gets done right and all the way. Commitment, determination, and pride: Not too many other combinations in life are as effective. Or as fulfilling.

Failure is not always a mistake. It may simply be the best one can do under the circumstances. The real mistake is to stop trying.[46]

– B.F. Skinner

Chapter 33

Pride, Honesty, and Peace of Mind

The *second* greatest impediment to a better life, from my perspective, is pride (the *greatest* impediment is fear, but we've discussed fear/courage already). Pride (ego, vanity, etc.) is very powerful, very common, very "human," and... *not good*. Pride, in so many ways, keeps us from leading the best life that we can.

Pride and ego sabotage many things in life that we could otherwise succeed in – I see it somewhere every day. *Relinquishing* our pride is a wise thing to do and is good for the mind and the soul. Relinquishing our pride is not weak and is *not* an act of passivity or submission. In fact, it is the very opposite. Relinquishing our pride is strong and courageous and healthy. When we surrender our ego, our mind can think purely, objectively, and without a self-serving agenda. Having unhealthy pride is like wearing glasses with lenses that make everything out in the world look the way we want it to, even though it is just self-deception. But pride also brings dishonesty to our dealings with others, because in and of itself, pride is dishonesty in the form of emotion and bias.

When we are prideful, when we let our ego and our vanity commandeer our thoughts and behaviors, we are choosing an illusion over truth. We *know* it's an illusion, but our ego simply won't let us admit it. Pride insists on keeping up appearances when, in fact, the appearances are a façade. Pride, thus, is a lie built for the purpose of ego protection – a lie that makes us feel better about ourselves, even though we know it is a deception that will never really hold up to scrutiny. When pride is removed, bias and the veneer of deception and vanity is removed, and our thoughts and actions become statements that we *truly* believe in and that can be trusted by others. *This* allows us peace of mind and harmony with others.

Here are some of the many ways that pride impedes our success, our honor, and our sense of peace:

- Pride wants to win an argument, to *defeat* another vs. viewing a *debate* as a way to better understand another's perspective
- Pride is fearful
- Pride prevents forgiveness because it wants a "pound of flesh" vs. reconciliation
- Pride prefers fear to respect and fear is not good for any relationship
- Pride would rather burn a bridge than concede error
- Pride prefers to lose a friendship vs. facing up to some embarrassment
- Pride is much more prone to anger than is humility
- Pride chooses ignorance over asking to be enlightened
- Pride chooses impasse over progress
- Pride makes excuses and blames others instead of taking responsibility
- Pride is defensive
- Pride is disingenuous
- Pride is off-putting, alienating
- Pride chooses sides based on agenda vs. principle
- Pride keeps us from being whom we want to be and, if allowed to persist, causes us to become something we don't want to be
- Pride is self-centered

The obvious question is how to keep from engaging in prideful behavior. Well, as with many things in life, the remedy is not easy, but it *is* simple: First, we must learn to be self-aware. We must be mindful of what we are saying and feeling and make sure that we believe in what we are saying and feeling to be genuine and true. Then, once we can be honest with ourselves and can acknowledge that we are wrong, we must do so in recognition of truth, fairness, objectivity, and often kindness.

As you conduct your day-to-day business, consider your perspectives and continue to ask yourself if pride is coloring your thoughts, feelings, and actions. Many times, it is. And *if* it is, ask yourself if surrendering it would not make your thoughts, feelings, and actions more pure, more honest, and more fair to others. Most of us say we want to live noble and honorable lives, but pride prevents this nobility by its very nature. Pride is a bad habit and a common one. But as with any bad habit, it can be broken. If you want to live a better, more successful, more honest, honorable, and peaceful life, become mindful of how much pride influences how you live and compel yourself to remove it from your thinking and the emotional responses in your daily life. As soon as you do, you will find that your life really is happier and more peaceful. I'm sure to the skeptical, this sounds like nothing more than the empty rhetoric of a feel-good self-help book. But, 1) rhetoric doesn't help you; *and* 2) all you have to do is test it. It works. *You'll see.*

Pride costs us more than hunger, thirst, and cold.[47]
– Thomas Jefferson

Chapter 34

Gratitude

A close and philosophical friend sent me a very kind e-mail not long ago, thanking me for some things I had sent him. I will spare you the details of his sentiments, but they were thoughtful and appreciative, and, frankly, over-generous. But his note was truly heart-warming, and it made me very happy and grateful for him as a friend. The second point of his e-mail was to suggest that gratitude itself would be a good topic for me to write about at some point. I liked his recommendation very much, so here we are…

Gratitude is such a simple, kind, affirming, and loving human expression. It is also an act that very often has a disproportionately powerful impact in relation to the effort that was required to bestow it. As with a number of benevolences, gratitude is many things. It is kindness, thoughtfulness, appreciation, love, and, perhaps, most of all, *acknowledgement.* Which is why a discussion of gratitude contributes to the theme of mental health and happiness: because when we acknowledge someone's kindness, when we make someone feel good about themselves, it makes us feel good, too, and as you know from previous chapters, I love anything with reciprocal value. Simply put, gratitude has truly meaningful benefits to the receiver *and* to the giver.

Just as laughter, cheerfulness, and generosity tend to produce more of themselves, gratitude tends to produce more gratitude. Obviously not always, but it has the tendency to bring more goodwill into the midst of things than existed there before. It may not be exponential (or is *factorial* the more accurate term? I never remember…), but it is undoubtedly contagious, and whenever it occurs, it seems to spark other kindnesses within the circle of its influence. And that is because when people *feel* good, they tend to *act* good (yes, it should be "well," grammatically, but the prose is just not as appealing written the correct way).

I'm sure you've seen examples of how happiness and goodwill seem naturally to go hand-in-hand. When we are in a good mood, we are a bit nicer to the drive-thru employee or the phone representative that has had us on hold too long or the guy that suddenly just turned right in front of us. Being happy makes the world seem brighter, less ugly, more hopeful. Being happy is a wonderful state of being, and even though we can't *guarantee* happiness or *sustain* it in someone else merely with small gestures, there is no question in my mind that we can bring happiness to people when we express gratitude for what they have done for us. Gratitude is a gift to the giver, but it is also a gift to all those around us, because the chances are very good that our gratitude will spread thoughtfulness to others. Which is something that is *always* of great value, regardless of the season, regardless of the times. It's a very small thing with very big results.

The following excerpted e-mail, edited slightly for space, is one I received recently from another close friend. I want to share it with you for several reasons: It is well-written and illustrative of the principles and philosophies I have written about in this book; it is compelling in its depiction of what this person has been able to achieve emotionally with humility, open-mindedness, and a sincere desire to improve as a person; it is a poignant reminder that changing how we think and act *is* within our control; and, it is a lovely expression of gratitude:

"I wanted to share this short reflection with you, especially because you are referenced in the first few lines, and because I am so incredibly grateful for you for all the times you showed me a better way.

When I reflect on the past two years of transformation, I can place just how dark my thoughts and emotions were – and how I once gave in to them because I had not yet learned how not to. I remember your telling me, "You're not a roulette wheel – you have control…" It's just that sometimes the air can get polluted by my overthinking or anxious thoughts. But when that happens, I have learned to step away, to stop standing directly under those sources of pollution, and to find a cleaner, fresher perspective of life. Nothing falls apart if I pause and take a break.

Today I recognize that I create my own reality based on my perception. I choose how to live – whether it's through the lens of love and authentic freedom or something else. I have power over how I respond to what happens around me and within me. When something upsets me, it's not about the other person – no one can make me feel anything. The other person is just triggering an area inside of me that requires healing. Every conflict I feel inside I have the ability to resolve.

It took me a long time to understand that feelings aren't good or bad; they just are. There was a time when I felt my emotions were against me, and I would've done anything to escape myself and my thoughts. But today I see that my feelings are just helping me process the world around me and where I stand in it. I have the freedom to choose how I respond to any given situation, and that is the most exquisite truth there is.

There are still moments today when I feel low, when I feel overwhelmed by my anxious thoughts, or when I have a deep sadness for life. And that's okay. That's normal. That's a defining aspect of being human, of being alive. But the wonderful thing is, no matter how low I feel, I know it will pass. I have faith – and proof – that I will feel better. Because I am learning every day how to love and honor the dignity of where I am in this moment. I am learning what it means to hold space for myself without judgment, no matter what I feel.

As this person proves, self-improvement – physical, mental, or otherwise – is about change, and change is about choice, determination, and earnestness. If you want to feel differently about yourself or life, in general, all you have to do is decide and commit. It works, and *anyone* can do it. But back to gratitude…

This may not be high-level psychology, mid-level philosophy, or even *low-level* wisdom, but there are certain words, certain concepts that are always good and positive, no matter what the angle of perspective. Have you ever heard of anyone saying, *"I really don't think diligence is all that great"*? Do you think that anyone in the history of mankind ever uttered these words: *"There is just too much excellence in the world"*? Or, *"I wish she wasn't so sincere – her integrity is really off-putting"?* Not likely. Sure, there are a few things in life that can be viewed as either good or bad, but some things are just simply *good*, and gratitude is one of those. I don't know anyone that isn't welcoming of gratitude or that does not feel better after extending it.

> *Appreciation is a wonderful thing. It makes what is*
> *excellent in others belong to us as well.*[48]
>
> – Voltaire

> *Wear gratitude like a cloak, and it will feed*
> *every corner of your life.*[49]
>
> – Rumi

> *Let us be grateful to the people who make us happy;*
> *they are the charming gardeners who make our souls blossom.*[50]
>
> – Marcel Proust

> *Gratitude is a powerful catalyst for happiness.*
> *It's the spark that lights a fire of joy in your soul.*[51]
>
> – Amy Collette

> *Gratitude is the sign of noble souls.*[52]
>
> – Aesop

> *Gratitude bestows reverence... changing forever how*
> *we experience life and the world.*[53]
>
> – John Milton

Chapter 35

Holes In The Formula

I am sure there are many readers who are frustrated with my formula, who are asking perfectly reasonable questions, such as, *"But, what about family?" "What about God and religion?" "What about nature and art and music?" "Aren't these things necessary for a person to be happy, as well?" "Are these not holes in your formula?"*

As I began writing this book and further developing the formula itself, I analyzed happiness in terms of what I believe was the *least number of elements* that would enable someone to be happy, and I determined that any human, notwithstanding debilitating mental and/or physical health issues, could realize long-term happiness if they had just the five elements we have discussed. Some people *do* require family relationships in order to be happy. Some people *do* require a belief in God and the practice of religion in order to be happy. But some people do not. And *because* some people do not, I did not include these in the formula. But I assure you they were excluded for this reason alone and not because I do not believe they can precipitate happiness. Similarly, there are lots of people that would claim that they *"cannot live"* without nature, art, or music, for example. And I am sure that is true for them. But, again, I based my formula on components without which, in my opinion, happiness cannot be achieved. While art and music and religion and family, for example, are all aspects that contribute to many, *many* people's happinesses, I do not believe they are essential for *everyone*. Please know that I am not suggesting that these are not all good and wonderful things. I have no political, moral, or religious agenda *whatsoever* in saying this. I am merely trying to dissect for you the thought processes I used in choosing what to include and what not to.

Can a person be happy without a purpose? I suppose it is possible, but it seems very unlikely to me. Can a person be happy without courage? Can a person choose their way in life without courage? Can they truly feel free? I'm sure this one seems arguable, depending on one's interpretation of the word, but regardless of the definition of "courage," if a person lives in fear – whether long-term and philosophical or short-term and situational – that person cannot be happy. Can a person be happy without emotional balance? Almost by definition, *no*, one cannot. Can a person be happy without being kind to people and having other good ethics? Once again, I will concede that it may be *possible*, but I find it extremely unlikely. And, can a person be happy without self-acceptance? No. Absolutely not. Unequivocally, *no*. And although I am very happy to accept that there are many *other* factors that may make people happy, these five things are the ones I believe we *must* all have in order to realize a life of true and lasting happiness. This is how I came to my formula, but I am certainly open to criticism…

Chapter 36

A Salve for Emotional Pain

Emotional pain – heartache, extreme sadness, loss, rejection, whatever form emotional pain may come in – is a dreadful thing. It often hurts deeply and for long periods of time, and it can pull us away from others and even away from ourselves.

There are many ways that we react to emotional pain. Some people gravitate towards others and some withdraw, languishing in the pain alone, either ruminating on it, or doing their best to avoid thinking about it. Rumination is never good, so I won't spend any more time denouncing it. For its part, though, *withdrawal* is not much better and is a very common response – and in some ways, not an unreasonable one, in the strictest sense of the word. Withdrawing from the world, from something that has hurt us is as logical as moving away from an extreme heat source or a dangerous animal. Why would we want to remain close to either? But withdrawal, depending on the circumstances, of course, tends to make things worse, even though at the time, it often feels better (or just less painful) than being with people and staying engaged.

Withdrawal is a very common defense mechanism. It is something that we believe will help us cope with the sadness and hurt, and in some ways it does, but only in a very superficial way. If we avoid "life," if we aren't engaging with society, we can avoid further pain, we often believe. But there are a couple of things that are not very good about this strategy. The first is that it is only a very temporary remedy. The second is that it changes the way we interact with others (when we do have to interact) and the way in which we interact with ourselves. I am very sympathetic to those who are in pain, and I am sympathetic to those who choose to withdraw for the reasons stated. But there is a better way.

Instead of either *absorbing* the pain alone or just plain withdrawing from family and friends, one can refocus one's mind on others. When we feel hurt, it is often very helpful to try to get outside one's self.

Instead of ruminating and staying inside your own mind, focusing on things *outside* yourself is a good way to partially ease the pain. And one of the *very* best ways I have found to focus outwardly is by helping others.

Helping others brings about obvious benefits, but it is also therapeutic to the *helper* in that it provides a healthier environment on which to focus our minds and activity. A gentle word of caution, however: Just because *you* are in help mode doesn't mean the person you decide you want to help is in *recipient* mode. Not everyone welcomes help. Just be careful that your assistance will be welcomed by the person you hope to help.

Focusing on things outside yourself *is good*. Helping others *is good*. But you may ask, *"Isn't refocusing on others just another form of avoidance, no matter how well-intended?"* Yes, in a way it is. It is but a *band-aid*. But of all the band-aids there are for emotional pain, it is the best one I know of. And the fact that it is *just* a band-aid is okay for the moment because the *real* solution for the pain may take a while to take effect. So, while you are actively working to resolve the source of your distress, helping others is something you can do that makes you and the other person feel better until your sorrows can be addressed directly and fully, especially in the early stages of your suffering. Helping others can take many forms, of course – it need not be *impressive*. Many times, the most welcome type of help is the sincerity of the gesture itself.

Helping with someone's children, the house, or just visiting with them when they are down is much more meaningful than you might think. Time itself, as a gift, is a very generous one that most people truly appreciate. But let's say you are not yet at the point in your sadness where you can gather the energy to really help someone. That's okay. Send them a text, an e-mail, or – heaven-forbid, these days – a *hand-written letter*, just to let them know you are thinking about them. And always do your best when you *are* out in the world to be proactively kind and generous to people. Go out of your way to make others feel good with a smile, a compliment, or just a warm hello. This will have the same therapeutic effect as more dynamic assistance will. You can always "ramp up" later when you are more emotionally ready.

Being in extreme emotional pain is very demotivating. When we feel bad – regardless of the reason – we tend not to want to do much of anything. But, if you will commit to this practice of proactive kindness in earnest, it will ease your pain, and the effort you exert will be well worth the energy expended, no matter how reluctant you may feel initially. The key to reversing your disheartenment is to overcome it with a commitment to doing the opposite of what you want to do (which is usually nothing) and hoping it all goes away on its own. Committing to the practice of helping others will not *erase* the pain, but it *will* diminish it by refocusing your thoughts outside your own condition and by making someone else feel good, which typically results in *your* feeling better about yourself. Isn't this a bit gimmicky, you may ask? Perhaps a little. *But it works.*

Do your best to muster as much energy as you can during your time of anguish and focus it on others as much as you are able. Tell them something good about *them* or direct sincere sentiments to them regarding your wishes for their happiness. Not much is likely to make you feel better when you are in the throes of the pain anyway, so at a minimum, it is worth a try. Caring about others – in any form – *will* make you feel better, and it *will* help pass the time, which is important, because in instances of heartbreak, sorrow, and other forms of emotional suffering, besides doing what you can to resolve the pain psychologically, time is often one of the only other effective mechanisms for healing there is. Time and kindness – even when the first moves slowly and the second takes energy you may not think you have – *will* combine to form a psychological, philosophical, and perhaps even *metaphysical* salve that will work when almost nothing else seems to, especially when your emotional pain is at its peak.

Those who are happiest are those who do the most for others.[54]
– Booker T. Washington

The best way to find yourself is to lose
yourself in the service of others.[55]
– Mohandas Gandhi

Chapter 37

Free Bonus Chapter!

The following things also bring peace and happiness. They are admittedly a bit less philosophical, and perhaps less permanent, but they, *too*, will gladden your heart and will very often bring an extra dose of contentment to your life, even if only for a few moments.

- Pet a dog. Or a cat. Or a goat, a dolphin, an elephant, a ferret, a duck (yes, you can pet a duck), or whatever animal is nearby that appears to be friendly and somewhat domesticated. Mongooses (mongeese?), badgers, wolves, and other wild creatures do not like to be petted, *per se*, so please beware. The point is that animals are wonderful. And those that will let you pet them will make you feel good (and they will love it). Animals often bring out the best in us. They calm us. They bring out the gentle and nurturing side of us. They, ironically, often bring out the *humanity* in us, as well. *Pet an animal.* Spend some time with him/her. It will be worth every minute that you do. And should you want to work for bonus points, *adopt* a dog or cat… or a duck. Rescues facilities are *full* of animals that need people just like you. And if they can't make you just a little happier, well… it might be time to re-read this book…

- Buy some fresh flowers for your dining table. Flowers are one of the most beautiful things on this earth, I think, and they cannot help but bring about gladness. The next time you're at the grocery store, buy a bunch or two. They are less expensive than you think. They will brighten even the most already-bright home and will make you feel good every time you see them.

- Stretch. Yes, *stretch*. I'm not suggesting you necessarily join a yoga class or even watch a yoga video on YouTube. All I'm suggesting is that you take a few minutes to stretch your back and your hamstrings and whatever other parts feel like taut leather straps. Stretching isn't necessarily fun. It can even be painful. The key is to start very slowly so that it doesn't hurt very much and so that the pain does not cause you to be averse to doing it again. Nothing I know of feels better than muscles and tendons and ligaments following a light session of stretching. Stretching also has scientific and undeniable anti-aging benefits (please look it up). Stretch for three minutes. You'll see. If you will go *slow and easy*, you will want it to do it regularly and longer. It will give you more energy, more flexibility, less walking-around aches and pains, and you will feel younger. *All for free.*

- Buy some fresh fruit and/or some fresh vegetables. Buy some things you really like but haven't purchased in a while. Or buy some things you have *never* tried before. Have you had sugar snap peas lately? Ever? They're delicious. Bought any fresh strawberries in a while? Blueberries? Avocado, mango, kiwi fruit? Ever tried a rutabaga? Why not try one? The earth gives us so many, many wonderful things, but often our routines and responsibilities and stressors cause us to overlook some of the beautiful but simple gifts it gives us. Sometimes, in an effort to refocus and to decompress, it is helpful to change up the daily grind by doing something different, something simple, and something easy, and buying fresh fruit/vegetables, if you are not already in the habit of doing so, is one of those things (just like buying flowers) that can make you feel good for very little effort or money. Both are a very pleasant dose of edible mental health.

- Tip someone that society doesn't traditionally tip. The trash collectors that are sometimes forced to deal with your unwieldy and bizarre garbage items, the busboy, the restaurant hostess, or the person at the drive-thru are all good considerations for people you may not typically think to tip. They have hectic jobs, and have to deal with the often unruly public, so when the garbage collectors take everything you have left at the curb, but by regulations don't necessarily have to, or when the drive-thru attendant is exceptionally polite, articulate, and thorough on the intercom and then gets the order exactly right at the window, I often feel that a tip is in order. I know *"they are just doing their job,"* but it is a difficult one and doing it cheerfully and consistently is worthy of a compliment, which in and of itself is more than they usually get – but I like to top off the compliment with a monetary thank-you. Or buy someone dinner anonymously. Another thing that will make both parties feel good about themselves (and life and society) is buying someone's lunch or dinner at a restaurant. It could be anyone, but my preference is to do this for those that might appear to have less money than others. Young people, for instance, that look like they are out enjoying a rare "sit-down" meal at a decent restaurant, or an older couple living on Social Security, perhaps, that probably don't get to go out very much, or maybe a group of men or women that, by their attire, are likely working at jobs that do not pay very much.

I have, on occasion, been "betrayed" by the server who, with kind intentions but against my wishes, outed me before I could leave, so I have seen their faces when it is revealed that their bill has been paid. And, yes, it is admittedly fun and nice to see their reaction. But what I prefer far more is to pay for their meal, leave a generous tip, and leave long before they know what has happened. It makes them feel good and saves them money, obviously, but it also makes them feel good about humanity (presumably) in that they cannot help but realize that the person who bought their meal did it for no other reason than because they could, with nothing to gain from it personally, except for the incidental happiness one gets from being kind to a stranger. I keep gift cards for Amazon and Target in my car (OK, a 2004 super sweet Tahoe, but still...) just so I will be ready if I encounter someone who could use a smile and a morale boost, then, I look for opportunities to brighten someone's day.

- Go for a walk. You need not have anywhere to go and it need not be a long walk. But it feels good to get your blood circulating, to breathe the fresh air, to feel the breeze, to hear the birds, to see the trees. A walk won't necessarily change your life, but it will very often make you feel better by changing your mood just enough to make a difference.

- Write a letter. Yes, with a pen and paper. I know it's all but unheard of these days, but this, too, will make you feel better. The paper will feel good to the touch. Seeing your own handwriting will feel good. Making the effort to do this for a family member or friend will feel good. Even just putting a stamp on the envelope will make you feel good. Addressing the envelope (assuming you still remember how) will make you feel good. And if this ancient method of communication is just too absurd for you, then, by all means, write an e-mail. Both are excellent gestures and will be welcomed either way. Write your favorite uncle, a former teacher, or coach. Write your favorite boss, your niece, your brother, a former neighbor, or anyone else you care about. What makes others feel good will make you feel good, too.

- Polish your shoes. Get some polish at the grocery store, if you don't have some around the house, and make your shoes look 10 times better. Even if there is no pending occasion for which you need them, having them ready for the next occasion will make you feel good.

- Build something or make something. You don't have to be "crafty" (although it certainly doesn't hurt). I have no idea why making something with your hands makes you feel good, but it does. *It just does.*

- Venture into nature. Go on a hike, drive your car to a park, walk to some nearby "scenery." Not able to do any of these? *No problem.* Turn off the TV and open a window or two. Listen to the birds, smell the air, feel the breeze. You don't have to have the right shoes, or even be mobile for that matter, to reap the benefits of the outdoors. Nature is everywhere, and it is beautiful.

- Text a friend. Re-connect or just say hi. Let them know you were thinking of them.

- Buy a plant. Buy *several* plants. Plant those plants in your yard or pot them and put them where you can see them. I can't articulate exactly why this feels good, but I think it is probably because they are living and beautiful. Simple, yet powerful.

- And please remember to pet a duck. Because you *can* pet a duck (but not necessarily a badger).

Conclusion

Are you happy? I truly hope so. That is my wish for *all* people, but, undoubtedly, many of you reading this are not. If you aren't, ask yourself which element or elements of the formula are keeping you from your happiness. Have you yet to find your purpose in life? Do you have fears that are impeding you from being as effective as you could be and, thus, less happy? Do your emotions foil your happiness on a regular basis? Are you less kind and ethical than you could be? Do you not really like who you are, or is that the whole problem?

This world can be a wonderful place to live. Or, it can be an ugly place. And, it can be both at the same time – in varying percentages and to varying degrees. It really just depends on one's perspective. But even more important than perspective is one's treatment of this world, the way in which one *chooses* to navigate this life. Life itself is just life. It's how we travel through it that makes it what it is, and I believe that life favors the principled – those that follow a set of values and philosophies comprised of purpose, courage, emotional balance, kind and ethical behavior, and the wise and practical thinking that produces self-acceptance. Life is not easy. But living it well, successfully, and happily is *simple,* if you believe in these principles and *apply* them consistently as you conduct your daily affairs.

Look at the lives of just about any happy person you know and you will find that although they may not have a simple life – it may be very dynamic and "involved" – they live happily by living according to a few basic principles from which they rarely deviate. Whether rich or poor, world traveler or home-body, solitary individual or parent of a large family, owner of small corner store or CEO of a large company, *anyone* can be happy and have true emotional peace with very little effort – and very often *do* – if they commit themselves to living according to the five principles we have discussed. Sure, life can be difficult, but those who live life *well* find it much easier to navigate. They either work through these bad times or simply rise above them and live well *in spite of it all.* Of course, you can always find an exception here and there, but I am confident that if you observe things objectively, you will make the same observations that I have over the years. And, then, *double check* this observation by looking at the lives of those that are *unhappy* and see if you don't find that those individuals live by a very *different* set of values. What I am certain you will find – beyond the stark differences in their values – is that most of their lives are quite complicated (regardless of their actual lifestyles) because of the principles (or lack thereof) they live by, which are typically the *cause* of their complications.

If you have one of these unhappy lives, I am absolutely convinced that you *can* be happy, if you will pursue a life that is dedicated to your chosen purpose, to daily courage, to emotional balance, kindness/ethics, and to self-acceptance. All journeys – mental, emotional, spiritual, or physical – start the same way: with a first step – no, a first *page*. So, why not begin re-writing the new draft today?

The story of your life is not predestined, and what you are, what you feel, and what you may be going through today are not the final chapter. The story of your life is written each day, and each day is an opportunity to edit and revise as you go. While some plot twists are, admittedly, forced upon us by life, the majority of these are ones that we have created of our own free will. Even *more* importantly, however, is that those events that *are* handed to us by life can very often be turned in whatever new and healthier direction we choose. So, why not take charge of your life and begin crafting a new and improved narrative as soon as you put down this book. You have nothing to lose and only peace and happiness to gain.

Acknowledgements

The first person I want to thank is my excellent boss. When I asked him, in my capacity as the Employee Assistance Program (EAP) Coordinator for our office, if he would allow me to publish "mental health-focused essays" on our EAP website, he said yes without hesitation and enthusiastically encouraged the idea. He read them, commented on many of them to me personally, and further encouraged me by simply expressing an interest in the subject matter and in the service he believed I was providing our colleagues. Without his immediate and continued encouragement, I would not have felt so confident in writing many of the essays that ultimately became the core of this book. Thank you, sir. I appreciate you and your exceptional leadership.

I am also indebted to numerous close friends who discussed this project with me at length, provided recommendations, and recognized many opportunities for me to make it better. To my great friends Shaun Manning, Jan Bost, Cheryl, and KGP: Thank you for all the time you spent helping me with this, for your generous friendship, and for your dedication.

JDB, thank you for your fervent encouragement, your affectionate badgering, and your faithful support of these and other of my philosophies on life.

And to my brother and sister and my wonderful group of close friends (I am certain you know who you are), thank you for making my life much happier than it would have been had you not been with me all along the way.

Notes

1. Goodreads. (n.d.). Impact Quotes. https://www.goodreads.com.
2. Goodreads. (n.d.). Change Quotes. https://www.goodreads.com.
3. Ibid.
4. Goodreads. (n.d.) Fearless Quotes. https://www.goodreads.com.
5. BrainyQuote. (n.d.) Mahatma Gandhi Quotes. https://www.brainyquote.com.
6. BrainyQuote. (n.d.). Thucydides Quotes. https://www.brainyquote.com.
7. Goodreads. (n.d.). Virgil Quotes. https://www.goodreads.com.
8. Goodreads. (n.d.). Courage Quotes. https://www.goodreads.com.
9. Ibid.
10. Ibid.
11. Decision Innovation. (n.d.) Emotional Quotes Related to Decision Making. https://www.decision-making-solutions.com.
12. BrainyQuote. (n.d.) Stephen Sondheim Quotes. https://www.brainyquote.com.
13. John Bartlett. (1992) Bartlett's Familiar Quotations, 16th Edition. (Justin Kaplan, General Editor). (319:14).
14. Kidadl. (2022, July 8). 95+ Best Quotes To Make You Think. https://www.kidadl.com.
15. Lonczak, Heather S. (2018, October 2). 19 Self-Acceptance Quotes For Relating To Yourself In A Healthier Way. PositivePsychology. https://www.positivepsychology.com.
16. Economy, Peter. (n.d.) 17 Super Inspiring Quotes About Always Being Your Best Self. Inc. https://www.inc.com.
17. Barra, Mathias. (2020, April 26). Rare and Powerful Quotes About the Importance of Self-Awareness. Medium. https://www.medium.com.
18. Objectivity Quotes (n.d.). BrainyQuote. https://www.brainyquote.com.
19. Powell, John. (n.d.) 40 Team Communication Quotes to Inspire Your Team. Tameday. https://www.tameday.com.

20. Dahl, Daniel. (2022, April 29) Listening Quotes That Express the Importance of Listening. Everydaypower. https://www.everydaypower.com.
21. BrainyQuote. (n.d.) Alfred Lord Tennyson Quotes. https://www.brainyquote.com.
22. Pinterest. (n.d.) Lifehack. Clarke Coaching. (Pinterest). https://www.pinterest.com.
23. Goodreads. (n.d.) Passive-Aggressive Quotes. Original Source: Ashta Chaitanya [Ashta-deb]. Life Happens To Us: A True Story. [2018, January 31] https://www.goodreads.com.
24. BrainyQuote. (n.d.). William James Quotes. https://www.brainyquote.com.
25. Quotefancy. (n.d.). Mark Twain Quotes. https://www.quotefancy.com.
26. QuoteMaster. (n.d.). Roy E. Disney. https://www.quotemaster.org.
27. BrainyQuote. (n.d.). Jonathan Larson Quotes. https://www.brainyquote.com.
28. Goodreads. (n.d.). Apology Quotes. https://www.goodreads.com.
29. Quote Investigator. (n.d.). Original Source: Chaucer, Geoffrey. [1392] The Tale of Melibeus. Canterbury Tales. https://www.quoteinvestigator.com.
30. Sprankles, Julie. (2021, October 5). Feeling Burnt Out? Read These Quotes When You Need A Mental Reset. Scarymommy. https://www.scarymommy.com.
31. BrainyQuote. (n.d.). Alone Quotes. https://www.brainyquote.com.
32. AZquotes. (n.d.). Lewis B. Smedes Quotes. https://www.azquotes.com.
33. Andersen, Charlotte Hilton. (2022, March 16). 16 Quotes About Boundaries That Will Help You Say "No." The Healthy. https://www.thehealthy.com.
34. Picturequotes. (n.d.) Shiv Khera Quotes. https://www.picturequotes.com.
35. Quotefancy. (n.d.) Bruce Lee Quotes. https://www.quotefancy.com.

36. John Bartlett. (1992). Bartlett's Familiar Quotations, 16th Edition. (Justin Kaplan, General Editor). (629:1). Original Source: Jung, Carl Gustav. *Psychological Reflections: A Jung Anthology* [1953] p. 83: Collected Works. Vol. 4, The Theory of Psychoanalysis. [1913].

37. eNotes (n.d.) Civil Disobedience. https://www.enotes.com

38. Quotepark.com (n.d.) Original Source: Durant, Will. [1926]. The Story of Philosophy phrases quoted by Durant are from Aristotle. [340 BCE] Nichomachean Ethics, Book II, 4; Book 1, 7. https://www.quotepark.com.

39. Bhatt, Ananya. (2021, September 28). 90 Tough Love Quotes For Your Relationship. The Random Vibez. https://www.therandomvibez.com.

40. Quotefancy. (n.d). Sally Hogshead Quotes. https://www.quotefancy.com.

41. Haley, Eleanor. (n.d.) 64 Quotes About Grief, Coping and Life After Loss. What's Your Grief? https://www.whatsyourgrief.com.

42. Ibid.

43. BrainyQuote. (n.d.). Martin Luther King, Jr. Quotes. https://www.brainyquote.com

44. Pyne, Holly. (2014, June 5). 15 Pieces of Wisdom From Edgar Allen Poe's Work. Shortlist. Original Source: Poe, Edgar Allen. Mesmeric Revelation. https://www.shortlist.com.

45. Goodreads. (n.d.) Adversity Quotes. https://www.goodreads.com.

46. Demers, Jayson. (n.d.) 35 Quotes About Perseverance And Never Giving Up. Inc. https://www.inc.com.

47. Kidadl. (n.d.) Quotes About Pride. https://www.kidadl.com

48. Hall, Leah. (2021, August 23). 58 Gratitude Quotes To Bring Joy To Every Day. Country Living. https://www.countryliving.com

49. Ibid.

50. Ibid.

51. Ibid.

52. Ibid.

53. Ibid.
54. Ngo, Kevin. (n.d.) 55 Meaningful Quotes About Helping
    Others. MotivationalWellBeing.com.
    https://www.motivationalwellbeing.com.
55. Ibid.

Written Guarantee: *Assertiveness*

I, Kevin Unruh, guarantee that if you, the reader, will sincerely commit to a philosophy of well-mannered assertiveness (vs. passive-aggressiveness) by expressing how you feel as soon as you have had time to really assess how you feel, and commit to this practice every day and in very human interaction, the practice of assertiveness will become easier and easier over time.

Guarantee not enforceable in any state or by any federal agency.
For entertainment purposes only (the author thinks he's funny).

Written Guarantee: *Procrastination*

I, Kevin Unruh, guarantee that if you, the reader, will start on your list and not stop until you have completed at least your top three "chores," your happiness, sense of accomplishment, and calm will increase immediately.

CPSIA information can be obtained
at www.ICGtesting.com
Printed in the USA
BVHW040758020723
666669BV00001B/13